D0830305

THE ORIGINS OF THE
FEDERAL RESERVE

THE ORIGINS OF THE
FEDERAL RESERVE

—— by ——

MURRAY ROTHBARD

Ludwig von Mises Institute

Selected from

A History of Money and Banking in the United States: The Colonial Era to World War II

Ludwig von Mises Institute
518 West Magnolia Avenue
Auburn, Alabama 36832
www.mises.org

ISBN: 978-1-933550-47-3

Contents

SECTION ONE
The Progressive Movement. 7

SECTION TWO
Unhappiness with the National Banking System 11

SECTION THREE
The Beginnings of the "Reform" Movement:
The Indianapolis Monetary Convention 15

SECTION FOUR
The Gold Standard Act of 1900 and After. 33

SECTION FIVE
Charles A. Conant, Surplus Capital,
and Economic Imperialism 41

SECTION SIX
Conant, Monetary Imperialism,
and the Gold-Exchange Standard 53

SECTION SEVEN
Jacob Schiff Ignites the Drive for a Central Bank. 71

SECTION EIGHT
The Panic of 1907 and
Mobilization for a Central Bank 79

SECTION NINE
The Final Phase: Coping with the
Democratic Ascendancy 97

SECTION TEN
Conclusion. 103

The Progressive Movement

The Federal Reserve Act of December 23, 1913, was part and parcel of the wave of Progressive legislation, on local, state, and federal levels of government, that began about 1900. Progressivism was a bipartisan movement which, in the course of the first two decades of the twentieth century, transformed the American economy and society from one of roughly *laissez-faire* to one of centralized statism.

Until the 1960s, historians had established the myth that Progressivism was a virtual uprising of workers and farmers who, guided by a new generation of altruistic experts and intellectuals, surmounted fierce big business opposition in order to curb, regulate, and control what had been a system of accelerating monopoly in the late nineteenth century. A generation of research and scholarship, however, has now exploded that myth for all parts of the American polity, and it has become all too clear that the truth is the reverse of this well-worn fable. In contrast, what actually happened was that business became increasingly competitive during the late nineteenth century, and that various big-business interests, led by the powerful financial house of J.P. Morgan and Company,

Originally published as "The Origins of the Federal Reserve," *Quarterly Journal of Austrian Economics* 2, no. 3 (Fall): 3–51.—Ed.

had tried desperately to establish successful cartels on the free market. The first wave of such cartels was in the first large-scale business, railroads, and in every case, the attempt to increase profits, by cutting sales with a quota system and thereby to raise prices or rates, collapsed quickly from internal competition within the cartel and from external competition by new competitors eager to undercut the cartel. During the 1890s, in the new field of large-scale industrial corporations, big-business interests tried to establish high prices and reduced production via mergers, and again, in every case, the mergers collapsed from the winds of new competition. In both sets of cartel attempts, J.P. Morgan and Company had taken the lead, and in both sets of cases, the market, hampered though it was by high protective tariff walls, managed to nullify these attempts at voluntary cartelization.

It then became clear to these big-business interests that the only way to establish a cartelized economy, an economy that would ensure their continued economic dominance and high profits, would be to use the powers of government to establish and maintain cartels by coercion. In other words, to transform the economy from roughly *laissez-faire* to centralized and coordinated statism. But how could the American people, steeped in a long tradition of fierce opposition to government-imposed monopoly, go along with this program? How could the public's consent to the New Order be engineered?

Fortunately for the cartelists, a solution to this vexing problem lay at hand. Monopoly could be put over *in the name of* opposition to monopoly! In that way, using the rhetoric beloved by Americans, the *form* of the political economy could be maintained, while the *content* could be totally reversed. Monopoly had always been defined, in the popular parlance and among economists, as "grants of exclusive privilege" by the government. It was now simply redefined as "big business" or business competitive practices, such as price-cutting, so that regulatory commissions, from the Interstate Commerce Commission to the Federal Trade Commission to state insurance commissions, were lobbied for and staffed by big-business men from the regulated industry, all done in the name of curbing "big business monopoly" on the free market. In that way, the regulatory commissions could subsidize, restrict, and cartelize in the name of "opposing monopoly," as well as promoting the general welfare and national security. Once again, it was railroad monopoly that paved the way.

For this intellectual shell game, the cartelists needed the support of the nation's intellectuals, the class of professional opinion molders in society. The Morgans needed a smoke screen of ideology, setting forth the rationale and the apologetics for the New Order. Again, fortunately for them, the intellectuals were ready and eager for the new alliance. The enormous growth of intellectuals, academics, social scientists, technocrats, engineers, social workers, physicians, and occupational "guilds" of all types in the late nineteenth century led most of these groups to organize for a far greater share of the pie than they could possibly achieve on the free market. These intellectuals needed the State to license, restrict, and cartelize their occupations, so as to raise the incomes for the fortunate people already in these fields. In return for their serving as apologists for the new statism, the State was prepared to offer not only cartelized occupations, but also ever increasing and cushier jobs in the bureaucracy to plan and propagandize for the newly statized society. And the intellectuals were ready for it, having learned in graduate schools in Germany the glories of statism and organicist socialism, of a harmonious "middle way" between dog-eat-dog *laissez-faire* on the one hand and proletarian Marxism on the other. Instead, big government, staffed by intellectuals and technocrats, steered by big business and aided by unions organizing a subservient labor force, would impose a cooperative commonwealth for the alleged benefit of all.

Unhappiness with the
National Banking System

The previous big push for statism in America had occurred during the Civil War, when the virtual one-party Congress after secession of the South emboldened the Republicans to enact their cherished statist program under cover of the war. The alliance of big business and big government with the Republican Party drove through an income tax, heavy excise taxes on such sinful products as tobacco and alcohol, high protective tariffs, and huge land grants and other subsidies to transcontinental railroads. The overbuilding of railroads led directly to Morgan's failed attempts at railroad pools, and finally to the creation, promoted by Morgan and Morgan-controlled railroads, of the Interstate Commerce Commission in 1887. The result of that was the long secular decline of the railroads beginning before 1900. The income tax was annulled by Supreme Court action, but was reinstated during the Progressive period.

The most interventionary of the Civil War actions was in the vital field of money and banking. The approach toward hard money and free banking that had been achieved during the 1840s and 1850s was swept away by two pernicious inflationist measures of the wartime Republican administration. One was fiat money greenbacks, which depreciated by half by the middle of the Civil War, and were finally replaced by the gold standard after urgent pressure by hard-money Democrats, but not until 1879, some 14 full years after the end of the war. A second, and more lasting, intervention was the National Banking Acts of 1863, 1864, and 1865, which destroyed the issue of bank notes by state-chartered (or "state") banks by a prohibitory tax, and then monopolized the issue of bank notes in the hands of a few large, federally chartered "national banks," mainly centered on Wall Street. In a typical cartelization, national banks were compelled by law to accept each other's notes and demand deposits at par, negating the process by which the free market had previously been discounting the notes and deposits of shaky and inflationary banks.

In this way, the Wall Street–federal government establishment was able to control the banking system, and inflate the supply of notes and deposits in a coordinated manner.

But there were still problems. The national banking system provided only a halfway house between free banking and government central banking, and by the end of the nineteenth century, the Wall Street banks were becoming increasingly unhappy with the status quo. The centralization was only limited, and, above all, there was no governmental central bank to coordinate inflation, and to act as a lender of last resort, bailing out banks in trouble. No sooner had bank credit generated booms when they got into trouble and bank-created booms turned into recessions, with banks forced to contract their loans and assets and to deflate in order to save themselves. Not only that, but after the initial shock of the National Banking Acts, state banks had grown rapidly by pyramiding their loans and demand deposits on top of national bank notes. These state banks, free of the high legal capital requirements that kept entry restricted in national banking, flourished during the 1880s and 1890s and provided stiff competition for the national banks themselves. Furthermore, St. Louis and Chicago, after the 1880s, provided increasingly severe competition to Wall Street. Thus, St. Louis and Chicago bank deposits, which had been only 16 percent of the St. Louis, Chicago, and New York City total in 1880, rose to 33 percent of that total by 1912. All in all, bank clearings outside of New York City, which were 24 percent of the national total in 1882, had risen to 43 percent by 1913.

The complaints of the big banks were summed up in one word: "inelasticity." The national banking system, they charged, did not provide for the proper "elasticity" of the money supply; that is, the banks were not able to expand money and credit as much as they wished, particularly in times of recession. In short, the national banking system did not provide sufficient room for inflationary expansions of credit by the nation's banks.[1]

By the turn of the century the political economy of the United States was dominated by two generally clashing financial aggregations: the previously dominant Morgan group, which had begun in investment banking and expanded into commercial banking, railroads, and mergers of manufacturing firms; and the Rockefeller forces, which began in oil refining

---

[1] On the national banking system background and on the increasing unhappiness of the big banks, see Murray N. Rothbard, "The Federal Reserve as a Cartelization Device: The Early Years, 1913–1920," in *Money in Crisis*, Barry Siegel, ed. (San Francisco: Pacific Institute, 1984), pp. 89–94; Ron Paul and Lewis Lehrman, *The Case for Gold: A Minority Report on the U.S. Gold Commission* (Washington, D.C.: Cato Institute, 1982); and Gabriel Kolko, *The Triumph of Conservatism: A Reinterpretation of American History* (Glencoe, Ill.: Free Press, 1983), pp. 139–46.

and then moved into commercial banking, finally forming an alliance with the Kuhn, Loeb Company in investment banking and the Harriman interests in railroads.[2]

Although these two financial blocs usually clashed with each other, they were as one on the need for a central bank. Even though the eventual major role in forming and dominating the Federal Reserve System was taken by the Morgans, the Rockefeller and Kuhn, Loeb forces were equally enthusiastic in pushing, and collaborating on, what they all considered to be an essential monetary reform.

---

[2] Indeed, much of the political history of the United States from the late nineteenth century until World War II may be interpreted by the closeness of each administration to one of these sometimes cooperating, more often conflicting, financial groupings: Cleveland (Morgan), McKinley (Rockefeller), Theodore Roosevelt (Morgan), Taft (Rockefeller), Wilson (Morgan), Harding (Rockefeller), Coolidge (Morgan), Hoover (Morgan), and Franklin Roosevelt (Harriman-Kuhn, Loeb-Rockefeller).

The Beginnings of the "Reform"
Movement: The Indianapolis Monetary
Convention

The presidential election of 1896 was a great national referendum on the gold standard. The Democratic Party had been captured, at its 1896 convention, by the Populist, ultra-inflationist, anti-gold forces, headed by William Jennings Bryan. The older Democrats, who had been fiercely devoted to hard money and the gold standard, either stayed home on election day or voted, for the first time in their lives, for the hated Republicans. The Republicans had long been the party of prohibition and of greenback inflation and opposition to gold. But since the early 1890s, the Rockefeller forces, dominant in their home state of Ohio and nationally in the Republican Party, had decided to quietly ditch prohibition as a political embarrassment and as a grave deterrent to obtaining votes from the increasingly powerful bloc of German-American voters. In the summer of 1896, anticipating the defeat of the gold forces at the Democratic convention, the Morgans, previously dominant in the Democratic Party, approached the McKinley-Mark Hanna-Rockefeller forces through their rising young satrap, Congressman Henry Cabot Lodge of Massachusetts. Lodge offered the Rockefeller forces a deal: The Morgans would support McKinley for president and neither sit home nor back a third, Gold Democrat party, provided that McKinley pledged himself to a gold standard. The deal was struck, and many previously hard-money Democrats shifted to the Republicans. The nature of the American political party system was now drastically changed: previously a tightly fought struggle between hard-money, free-trade, *laissez-faire* Democrats on the one hand, and protectionist, inflationist, and statist Republicans on the other, with the Democrats slowly but surely gaining ascendancy by the early 1890s, was now a party system that would be dominated by the Republicans until the depression election of 1932.

The Morgans were strongly opposed to Bryanism, which was not only Populist and inflationist, but also anti-Wall Street bank; the Bryanites, much like Populists of the present day, preferred congressional, greenback inflationism to the more subtle, and more privileged, big-bank-controlled variety. The Morgans, in contrast, favored a gold standard. But, once gold was secured by the McKinley victory of 1896, they wanted to press on to use the gold standard as a hard-money camouflage behind which they could change the system into one less nakedly inflationist than populism but far more effectively controlled by the big-banker elites. In the long run, a controlled Morgan-Rockefeller gold standard was far more pernicious to the cause of genuine hard money than a candid free-silver or greenback Bryanism.

As soon as McKinley was safely elected, the Morgan-Rockefeller forces began to organize a "reform" movement to cure the "inelasticity" of money in the existing gold standard and to move slowly toward the establishment of a central bank. To do so, they decided to use the techniques they had successfully employed in establishing a pro-gold standard movement during 1895 and 1896. The crucial point was to avoid the public suspicion of Wall Street and banker control by acquiring the patina of a broad-based grassroots movement. To do so, the movement was deliberately focused in the Middle West, the heartland of America, and organizations developed that included not only bankers, but also businessmen, economists, and other academics, who supplied respectability, persuasiveness, and technical expertise to the reform cause.

Accordingly, the reform drive began just after the 1896 elections in authentic Midwest country. Hugh Henry Hanna, president of the Atlas Engine Works of Indianapolis, who had learned organizing tactics during the year with the pro-gold standard Union for Sound Money, sent a memorandum, in November, to the Indianapolis Board of Trade, urging a grassroots Midwestern state like Indiana to take the lead in currency reform.[3]

In response, the reformers moved fast. Answering the call of the Indianapolis Board of Trade, delegates from boards of trade from 12 Midwestern cities met in Indianapolis on December 1, 1896. The conference called for a large monetary convention of businessmen, which accordingly met in Indianapolis on January 12, 1897. Representatives from 26 states and the District of Columbia were present. The monetary reform movement was now officially under way. The influential *Yale Review* commended the convention for averting the danger of arousing popular hostility to bankers. It reported that "the conference was a gathering of businessmen in general rather than bankers in particular."[4]

---

[3] For the memorandum, see James Livingston, *Origins of the Federal Reserve System: Money, Class, and Corporate Capitalism*, 1890–1913 (Ithaca, N.Y.: Cornell University Press, 1986), pp. 104–05.

[4] *Yale Review* 5 (1897): 343–45, quoted in ibid., p. 105.

The conventioneers may have been businessmen, but they were certainly not very grassrootsy. Presiding at the Indianapolis Monetary Convention of 1897 was C. Stuart Patterson, dean of the University of Pennsylvania Law School and a member of the finance committee of the powerful, Morgan-oriented Pennsylvania Railroad. The day after the convention opened, Hugh Hanna was named chairman of an executive committee which he would appoint. The committee was empowered to act for the convention after it adjourned. The executive committee consisted of the following influential corporate and financial leaders:

John J. Mitchell of Chicago, president of the Illinois Trust and Savings Bank, and a director of the Chicago and Alton Railroad; the Pittsburgh, Fort Wayne and Chicago Railroad; and the Pullman Company. Mitchell was named treasurer of the executive committee.

H.H. Kohlsaat, editor and publisher of the *Chicago Times-Herald* and the Chicago *Ocean Herald*, trustee of the Chicago Art Institute, and a friend and adviser of Rockefeller's main man in politics, President William McKinley.

Charles Custis Harrison, provost of the University of Pennsylvania, who had made a fortune as a sugar refiner in partnership with the powerful Havemeyer ("Sugar Trust") interests.

Alexander E. Orr, New York City banker in the Morgan ambit, who was a director of the Morgan-run Erie and Chicago, Rock Island, and Pacific Railroads; of the National Bank of Commerce; and of the influential publishing house, Harper Brothers. Orr was also a partner in the country's largest grain merchandising firm and a director of several life insurance companies.

Edwin O. Stanard, St. Louis grain merchant, former governor of Missouri, and former vice president of the National Board of Trade and Transportation.

E.B. Stahlman, owner of the *Nashville Banner*, commissioner of the cartelist Southern Railway and Steamship Association, and former vice president of the Louisville, New Albany, and Chicago Railroad.

A.E. Willson, influential attorney from Louisville and a future governor of Kentucky.

But the two most interesting and powerful executive committee members of the Indianapolis Monetary Convention were Henry C. Payne and George Foster Peabody. Henry Payne was a Republican Party leader from Milwaukee and president of the Morgan-dominated Wisconsin Telephone Company, long associated with the railroad-oriented Spooner-Sawyer Republican machine in Wisconsin politics. Payne was also heavily involved in Milwaukee utility and banking interests, in particular as a longtime director of the North American Company, a large public utility holding company headed by New York City financier Charles W. Wetmore. So close was North American to the Morgan interests that its board included two top Morgan financiers. One was Edmund C. Converse, president of Morgan-run Liberty National Bank of New York City, and soon-to-be founding president of Morgan's Bankers Trust Company. The other was Robert Bacon, a partner in J.P. Morgan and Company, and one of Theodore Roosevelt's closest friends, whom Roosevelt would make assistant secretary of state. Furthermore, when Theodore Roosevelt became president as the result of the assassination of William McKinley, he replaced Rockefeller's top political operative, Mark Hanna of Ohio, with Henry C. Payne as postmaster general of the United States. Payne, a leading Morgan lieutenant, was reportedly appointed to what was then the major political post in the Cabinet, specifically to break Hanna's hold over the national Republican Party. It seems clear that replacing Hanna with Payne was part of the savage assault that Theodore Roosevelt would soon launch against Standard Oil as part of the open warfare about to break out between the Rockefeller-Harriman-Kuhn, Loeb camp and the Morgan camp.[5]

Even more powerful in the Morgan ambit was the secretary of the Indianapolis Monetary Convention's executive committee, George Foster Peabody. The entire Peabody family of Boston Brahmins had long been personally and financially closely associated with the Morgans. A member of the Peabody clan had even served as best man at J.P. Morgan's wedding in 1865. George Peabody had long ago established an international banking firm of which J.P. Morgan's father, Junius, had been one of the senior partners. George Foster Peabody was an eminent New York investment banker with extensive holdings in Mexico, who was to help reorganize General Electric for the Morgans, and was later offered the job of secretary of the Treasury during the Wilson administration. He would function throughout that administration as a "statesman without portfolio."[6]

Let the masses be hoodwinked into regarding the Indianapolis Monetary Convention as a spontaneous grassroots outpouring of small Midwestern businessmen. To the *cognoscenti*, any organization featuring Henry Payne, Alexander Orr, and especially George Foster Peabody meant but one thing: J.P. Morgan.

The Indianapolis Monetary Convention quickly resolved to urge President McKinley to (1) continue the gold standard, and (2) create a new system of "elastic" bank credit.

---

[5] See Philip H. Burch, Jr., *Elites in American History*, vol. 2, *The Civil War to the New Deal* (New York:Holmes and Meier, 1981), p. 189, n. 55.

[6] Ibid., pp. 231, 233. See also Louise Ware, *George Foster Peabody* (Athens: University of Georgia Press, 1951), pp. 161–67.

To that end, the convention urged the president to appoint a new monetary commission to prepare legislation for a new revised monetary system. McKinley was very much in favor of the proposal, signaling Rockefeller agreement, and on July 24 he sent a message to Congress urging the creation of a special monetary commission. The bill for a national monetary commission passed the House of Representatives but died in the Senate.[7]

Disappointed but intrepid, the executive committee, failing a presidentially appointed commission, decided in August 1897 to go ahead and select its own. The leading role in appointing this commission was played by George Foster Peabody, who served as liaison between the Indianapolis members and the New York financial community. To select the commission members, Peabody arranged for the executive committee to meet in the Saratoga Springs summer home of his investment banking partner, Spencer Trask. By September, the executive committee had selected the members of the Indianapolis Monetary Commission.

The members of the new Indianapolis Monetary Commission were as follows:[8]

Chairman was former Senator George F. Edmunds, Republican of Vermont, attorney, and former director of several railroads.

C. Stuart Patterson, dean of University of Pennsylvania Law School, and a top official of the Morgan-controlled Pennsylvania Railroad.

---

[7] See Kolko, *Triumph*, pp. 147–48.

[8] See Livingston, *Origins*, pp. 106–07.

Charles S. Fairchild, a leading New York banker, president of the New York Security and Trust Company, former partner in the Boston Brahmin investment banking firm of Lee, Higginson and Company, and executive and director of two major railroads. Fairchild, a leader in New York state politics, had been secretary of the Treasury in the first Cleveland administration. In addition, Fairchild's father, Sidney T. Fairchild, had been a leading attorney for the Morgan-controlled New York Central Railroad.

Stuyvesant Fish, scion of two longtime aristocratic New York families, was a partner of the Morgan-dominated New York investment bank of Morton, Bliss and Company, and then president of Illinois Central Railroad and a trustee of Mutual Life. Fish's father had been a senator, governor, and secretary of state.

Louis A. Garnett was a leading San Francisco businessman.

Thomas G. Bush of Alabama was a director of the Mobile and Birmingham Railroad.

J.W. Fries was a leading cotton manufacturer from North Carolina.

William B. Dean was a merchant from St. Paul, Minnesota, and a director of the St. Paul–based transcontinental Great Northern Railroad, owned by James J. Hill, ally with Morgan in the titanic struggle over the Northern Pacific Railroad with Harriman, Rockefeller, and Kuhn, Loeb.

George Leighton of St. Louis was an attorney for the Missouri Pacific Railroad.

Robert S. Taylor was an Indiana patent attorney for the Morgan-controlled General Electric Company.

The single most important working member of the commission was James Laurence Laughlin, head professor of political economy at the new Rockefeller-founded University of Chicago and editor of its prestigious *Journal of Political Economy*. It was Laughlin who supervised the operations of the commission's staff and the writing of the reports. Indeed, the two staff assistants to the commission who wrote reports were both students of Laughlin's at Chicago: former student L. Carroll Root, and his current graduate student Henry Parker Willis.

The impressive sum of $50,000 was raised throughout the nation's banking and corporate community to finance the work of the Indianapolis Monetary Commission. New York City's large quota was raised by Morgan bankers Peabody and Orr, and heavy contributions to fill the quota came promptly from mining magnate William E. Dodge; cotton and coffee trader Henry Hentz, a director of the Mechanics National Bank; and J.P. Morgan himself.

With the money in hand, the executive committee rented office space in Washington, D.C., in mid-September, and set the staff to sending out and collating the replies to a detailed monetary questionnaire, sent to several hundred selected experts. The monetary commission sat from late September into December 1897, sifting through the replies to the questionnaire collated by Root and Willis. The purpose of the questionnaire was to mobilize a broad base of support for the commission's recommendations, which they could claim represented hundreds of expert views. Second, the questionnaire served as an important public relations device, making the commission and its work highly visible to the public, to the business community throughout the country, and to members of Congress. Furthermore, through this device, the commission could be seen as speaking for the business community throughout the country.

To this end, the original idea was to publish the Indianapolis Monetary Commission's preliminary report, adopted in mid-December, as well as the questionnaire replies in a companion volume. Plans for the questionnaire volume fell through, although it was later published as part of a series of publications on political economy and public law by the University of Pennsylvania.[9]

Undaunted by the slight setback, the executive committee developed new methods of molding public opinion using the questionnaire replies as an organizing tool. In November, Hugh Hanna hired as his Washington assistant financial journalist Charles A. Conant, whose task was to propagandize and organize public opinion for the recommendations of the commission. The campaign to beat the drums for the forthcoming commission report was launched when Conant published an article in the December 1 issue of *Sound Currency* magazine, taking an advanced line on the report, and bolstering the conclusions not only with his own knowledge of monetary and banking history, but also with frequent statements from the as-yet-unpublished replies to the staff questionnaire.

Over the next several months, Conant worked closely with Jules Guthridge, the general secretary of the commission; they first induced newspapers throughout the country to print abstracts of the questionnaire replies. As Guthridge wrote some commission members, he thereby stimulated "public curiosity" about the forthcoming report, and he boasted that by "careful manipulation" he was able to get the preliminary report "printed in whole or in part—principally in part—in nearly 7,500 newspapers, large and small." In the meanwhile, Guthridge and Conant orchestrated letters of support from prominent men across the country, when the preliminary report

---

[9] See Livingston, *Origins*, pp. 107–08.

was published on January 3, 1898. As soon as the report was published, Guthridge and Conant made these letters available to the daily newspapers. Quickly, the two built up a distribution system to spread the gospel of the report, organizing nearly 100,000 correspondents "dedicated to the enactment of the commission's plan for banking and currency reform."[10]

The prime and immediate emphasis of the preliminary report of the Indianapolis Monetary Commission was to complete the promise of the McKinley victory by codifying and enacting what was already in place de facto: a single gold standard, with silver reduced to the status of subsidiary token currency. Completing the victory over Bryanism and free silver, however, was just a mopping-up operation; more important in the long run was the call raised by the report for banking reform to allow greater elasticity. Bank credit could then be increased in recessions and whenever seasonal pressure for redemption by agricultural country banks forced the large central reserve banks to contract their loans. The actual measures called for by the commission were of marginal importance. (More important was that the question of banking reform had been raised at all.)

The public having been aroused by the preliminary report, the executive committee decided to organize a second and final meeting of the Indianapolis Monetary Convention, which duly met at Indianapolis on January 25, 1898. The second convention was a far grander affair than the first, bringing together 496 delegates from 31 states. Furthermore, the gathering was a cross-section of America's top corporate leaders. While the state of Indiana naturally had the largest delegation, of 85 representatives of boards of trade and chambers of commerce, New York sent 74 delegates, including many from the Board

---

[10] Ibid., pp. 109–10.

of Trade and Transportation, the Merchants' Association, and the Chamber of Commerce in New York City.

Such corporate leaders attended as Cleveland iron manufacturer Alfred A. Pope, president of the National Malleable Castings Company; Virgil P. Cline, legal counsel to Rockefeller's Standard Oil Company of Ohio; and C.A. Pillsbury of Minneapolis-St. Paul, organizer of the world's largest flour mills. From Chicago came such business notables as Marshall Field and Albert A. Sprague, a director of the Chicago Telephone Company, subsidiary of the Morgan-controlled telephone monopoly, American Telephone and Telegraph Company. Not to be overlooked was delegate Franklin MacVeagh, a wholesale grocer from Chicago, and an uncle of a senior partner in the Wall Street law firm of Bangs, Stetson, Tracy and MacVeagh, counsel to J.P. Morgan and Company. MacVeagh, who was later to become secretary of the Treasury in the Taft administration, was wholly in the Morgan ambit. His fatherin-law, Henry F. Eames, was the founder of the Commercial National Bank of Chicago, and his brother Wayne was soon to become a trustee of the Morgan-dominated Mutual Life Insurance Company.

The purpose of the second convention, as former Secretary of the Treasury Charles S. Fairchild candidly explained in his address to the gathering, was to mobilize the nation's leading businessmen into a mighty and influential reform movement. As he put it, "If men of business give serious attention and study to these subjects, they will substantially agree upon legislation, and thus agreeing, their influence will be prevailing." He concluded, "My word to you is, pull all together." Presiding officer of the convention, Iowa Governor Leslie M. Shaw, was, however, a bit disingenuous when he told the gathering, "You represent today not the banks, for there are few bankers on this floor. You represent the business industries and the financial interests of the country." There were plenty of bankers there, too.[11] Shaw himself, later to be secretary of the Treasury under Theodore Roosevelt, was a small-town banker in Iowa, and president of the Bank of Denison who continued as bank president throughout his term as convention governor. More important in Shaw's outlook and career was the fact that he was a longtime close friend and loyal supporter of the Des Moines Regency, the Iowa Republican machine headed by the powerful Senator William Boyd Allison. Allison, who was to obtain the Treasury post for his friend, was in turn tied closely to Charles E. Perkins, a close Morgan ally, president of the Chicago, Burlington and Quincy Railroad, and kinsman of the powerful Forbes financial group of Boston, long tied in with the Morgan interests.[12]

Also serving as delegates to the second convention were several eminent economists, each of whom, however, came not as academic observers but as representatives of elements of the business community. Professor Jeremiah W. Jenks of Cornell, a proponent of trust cartelization by government and soon to become a friend and adviser of Theodore Roosevelt as governor, came as delegate from the Ithaca Business Men's Association. Frank W. Taussig of Harvard University represented the Cambridge Merchants' Association. Yale's Arthur Twining Hadley, soon to be the president of Yale, represented the New Haven Chamber of Commerce, and Frank M. Taylor of the University of Michigan came as representative of the Ann Arbor Business Men's Association. Each of these men held powerful posts in the organized economics profession, Jenkins, Taussig, and Taylor serving on the currency committee of the

---

[11] Ibid., pp. 113–15.

[12] See Rothbard, "Federal Reserve," pp. 95–96.

American Economic Association. Hadley, a leading railroad economist, also served on the boards of directors of Morgan's New York, New Haven and Hartford and Atchison, Topeka and Santa Fe Railroads.[13]

Both Taussig and Taylor were monetary theorists who, while committed to a gold standard, urged reform that would make the money supply more elastic. Taussig called for an expansion of national bank notes, which would inflate in response to the "needs of business." As Taussig[14] put it, the currency would then "grow without trammels as the needs of the community spontaneously call for increase." Taylor, too, as one historian puts it, wanted the gold standard to be modified by "a conscious control of the movement of money" by government "in order to maintain the stability of the credit system." Taylor justified governmental suspensions of specie payment to "protect the gold reserve."[15]

On January 26, the convention delegates duly endorsed the preliminary report with virtual unanimity, after which Professor J. Laurence Laughlin was assigned the task of drawing up a more elaborate final report, which was published and

---

[13] On Hadley, Jenks, and especially Conant, see Carl P. Parrini and Martin J. Sklar, "New Thinking about the Market, 1896–1904: Some American Economists on Investment and the Theory of Surplus Capital," *Journal of Economic History* 43 (September 1983): 559–78. The authors point out that Conant's and Hadley's major works of 1896 were both published by G.P. Putnam's Sons of New York. President of Putnam's was George Haven Putnam, a leader in the new banking reform movement. Ibid., p. 561, n. 2.

[14] Frank W. Taussig, "What Should Congress Do About Money?" *Review of Reviews* (August 1893): 151, quoted in Joseph Dorfman, *The Economic Mind in American Civilization* (New York: Viking Press, 1949), 3, p. xxxvii. See also ibid., p. 269.

[15] Ibid., pp. 392–93.

distributed a few months later. Laughlin's—and the convention's— final report not only came out in favor of a broadened asset base for a greatly increased amount of national bank notes, but also called explicitly for a central bank that would enjoy a monopoly of the issue of bank notes.[16]

The convention delegates took the gospel of banking reform to the length and breadth of the corporate and financial communities. In April 1898, for example, A. Barton Hepburn, president of the Chase National Bank of New York, at that time a flagship commercial bank for the Morgan interests and a man who would play a large role in the drive to establish a central bank, invited Indianapolis Monetary Commissioner Robert S. Taylor to address the New York State Bankers Association on the currency question, since "bankers, like other people, need instruction upon this subject." All the monetary commissioners, especially Taylor, were active during the first half of 1898 in exhorting groups of businessmen throughout the nation for monetary reform.

Meanwhile, in Washington, the lobbying team of Hanna and Conant was extremely active. A bill embodying the suggestions of the monetary commission was introduced by Indiana Congressman Jesse Overstreet in January, and was reported out by the House Banking and Currency Committee in May. In the meantime, Conant met almost continuously with the banking committee members. At each stage of the legislative process,

---

[16] The final report, including its recommendations for a central bank, was hailed by F.M. Taylor, in his "The Final Report of the Indianapolis Monetary Commission," *Journal of Political Economy* 6 (June 1898): 293–322. Taylor also exulted that the convention had been "one of the most notable movements of our time—the first thoroughly organized movement of the business classes in the whole country directed to the bringing about of a radical change in national legislation." Ibid., p. 322.

Hanna sent letters to the convention delegates and to the public, urging a letter-writing campaign in support of the bill.

In this agitation, McKinley Secretary of the Treasury Lyman J. Gage worked closely with Hanna and his staff. Gage sponsored similar bills, and several bills along the same lines were introduced in the House in 1898 and 1899. Gage, a friend of several of the monetary commissioners, was one of the top leaders of the Rockefeller interests in the banking field. His appointment as Treasury secretary had been gained for him by Ohio's Mark Hanna, political mastermind and financial backer of President McKinley, and old friend, high-school classmate, and business associate of John D. Rockefeller, Sr. Before his appointment to the cabinet, Gage was president of the powerful First National Bank of Chicago, one of the major commercial banks in the Rockefeller ambit. During his term in office, Gage tried to operate the Treasury as a central bank, pumping in money during recessions by purchasing government bonds on the open market, and depositing large funds with pet commercial banks. In 1900, Gage called vainly for the establishment of regional central banks.

Finally, in his last annual report as secretary of the Treasury in 1901, Lyman Gage let the cat completely out of the bag, calling outright for a government central bank. Without such a central bank, he declared in alarm, "individual banks stand isolated and apart, separated units, with no tie of mutuality between them." Unless a central bank established such ties, Gage warned, the panic of 1893 would be repeated.[17] When he left office early the next year, Lyman Gage took

---

[17] Livingston, *Origins*, p. 153.

up his post as president of the Rockefeller-controlled U.S. Trust Company in New York City.[18]

---

[18] Rothbard, "Federal Reserve," pp. 94–95.

The Gold Standard Act of 1900 and After

Any reform legislation had to wait until after the elections of 1898, for the gold forces were not yet in control of Congress. In the autumn, the executive committee of the Indianapolis Monetary Convention mobilized its forces, calling on no less than 97,000 correspondents throughout the country through whom it had distributed the preliminary report. The executive committee urged its constituency to elect a gold-standard Congress; when the gold forces routed the silverites in November, the results of the election were hailed by Hanna as eminently satisfactory.

The decks were now cleared for the McKinley administration to submit its bill, and the Congress that met in December 1899 quickly passed the measure; Congress then passed the conference report of the Gold Standard Act in March 1900.

The currency reformers had gotten their way. It is well known that the Gold Standard Act provided for a single gold standard, with no retention of silver money except as tokens. Less well known are the clauses that began the march toward a more "elastic" currency. As Lyman Gage had suggested in 1897, national banks, previously confined to large cities, were now made possible with a small amount of capital in small towns and rural areas. And it was made far easier for national banks to issue notes. The object of these clauses, as one historian put it, was to satisfy an "increased demand for money at crop-moving time, and to meet popular cries for 'more money' by encouraging the organization of national banks in comparatively undeveloped regions."[19]

The reformers exulted over the passage of the Gold Standard Act, but took the line that this was only the first step on the much-needed path to fundamental banking reform. Thus, Professor Frank W. Taussig of Harvard praised the act, and greeted the emergence of a new social and ideological alignment, caused by "strong pressure from the business community" through the Indianapolis Monetary Convention. He particularly welcomed the fact that the Gold Standard Act "treats the national banks not as grasping and dangerous corporations but as useful institutions deserving the fostering care of the legislature." But such tender legislative care was not enough; fundamental banking reform was needed. For, Taussig declared, "The changes in banking legislation are not such as to make possible any considerable expansion of the national system or to enable it to render the community the full service of which it is capable." In short, the changes allowed for more and greater expansion of bank credit and the supply of money. Therefore, Taussig concluded, "It is well nigh certain that eventually Congress will have to consider once more the further remodeling of the national bank system."[20]

In fact, the Gold Standard Act of 1900 was only the opening gun of the banking reform movement. Three friends and financial journalists, two from Chicago, were to play a large role in the development of that movement. Massachusetts-born

---

[19] Livingston, *Origins*, p. 123

[20] Frank W. Taussig, "The Currency Act of 1900," *Quarterly Journal of Economics* 14 (May 1900): 415.

Charles A. Conant (1861–1915), a leading historian of banking, wrote *A History of Modern Banks of Issue* in 1896, while still a Washington correspondent for the *New York Journal of Commerce* and an editor of *Bankers Magazine*. After his stint of public relations work and lobbying for the Indianapolis convention, Conant moved to New York in 1902 to become treasurer of the Morgan-oriented Morton Trust Company. The two Chicagoans, both friends of Lyman Gage, were, along with Gage, in the Rockefeller ambit: Frank A. Vanderlip was picked by Gage as his assistant secretary of the Treasury, and when Gage left office, Vanderlip came to New York as a top executive at the flagship commercial bank of the Rockefeller interests, the National City Bank of New York. Meanwhile, Vanderlip's close friend and mentor at the *Chicago Tribune*, Joseph French Johnson, had also moved east to become professor of finance at the Wharton School of the University of Pennsylvania. But no sooner had the Gold Standard Act been passed when Joseph Johnson sounded the trump by calling for more fundamental reform.

Professor Johnson stated flatly that the existing bank note system was weak in not "responding to the needs of the money market," that is, not supplying a sufficient amount of money. Since the national banking system was incapable of supplying those needs, Johnson opined, there was no reason to continue it. Johnson deplored the U.S. banking system as the worst in the world, and pointed to the glorious central banking system as existed in Britain and France.[21] But no such centralized banking system yet existed in the United States:

---

[21] Joseph French Johnson, "The Currency Act of March 14, 1900," *Political Science Quarterly* 15 (1900): 482–507. Johnson, however, deplored the one fly in the Bank of England ointment—the remnant

> In the United States, however, there is no single business
> institution, and no group of large institutions, in which
> self-interest, responsibility, and power naturally unite and
> conspire for the protection of the monetary system against
> twists and strains.

In short, there was far too much freedom and decentralization in the system. In consequence, our massive deposit credit
system "trembles whenever the foundations are disturbed,"
that is, whenever the chickens of inflationary credit expansion
came home to roost in demands for cash or gold. The result of
the inelasticity of money, and of the impossibility of interbank
cooperation, Johnson opined, was that we were in danger of
losing gold abroad just at the time when gold was needed to
sustain confidence in the nation's banking system.[22]

After 1900, the banking community was split on the question of reform, the small and rural bankers preferring the status
quo. But the large bankers, headed by A. Barton Hepburn of
Morgan's Chase National Bank, drew up a bill as head of a
commission of the American Bankers Association, and presented it in late 1901 to Representative Charles N. Fowler of
New Jersey, chairman of the House Banking and Currency
Committee, who had introduced one of the bills that had led
to the Gold Standard Act. The Hepburn proposal was reported
out of committee in April 1902 as the Fowler Bill.[23]

The Fowler Bill contained three basic clauses. One allowed
the further expansion of national bank notes based on broader
assets than government bonds. The second, a favorite of the

---

of the hard- money Peel's Bank Act of 1844 that placed restrictions
on the quantity of bank note issue. Ibid., p. 496.

[22] Ibid., pp. 497f.

[23] Kolko, *Triumph*, pp. 149–50.

big banks, was to allow national banks to establish branches at home and abroad, a step illegal under the existing system due to fierce opposition by the small country bankers. While branch banking is consonant with a free market and provides a sound and efficient system for calling on other banks for redemption, the big banks had little interest in branch banking unless accompanied by centralization of the banking system. Thus, the Fowler Bill proposed to create a three-member board of control within the Treasury Department to supervise the creation of the new bank notes and to establish clearinghouse associations under its aegis. This provision was designed to be the first step toward the establishment of a full-fledged central bank.[24]

Although they could not control the American Bankers Association, the multitude of country bankers, up in arms against the proposed competition of big banks in the form of branch banking, put fierce pressure upon Congress and managed to kill the Fowler Bill in the House during 1902, despite the agitation of the executive committee and staff of the Indianapolis Monetary Convention.

With the defeat of the Fowler Bill, the big bankers decided to settle for more modest goals for the time being. Senator Nelson W. Aldrich of Rhode Island, perennial Republican leader of the U.S. Senate and Rockefeller's man in Congress,[25] submitted the Aldrich Bill the following year, allowing the large national banks in New York to issue "emergency

---

[24] See Livingston, *Origins*, pp. 150–54.

[25] Nelson W. Aldrich, who entered the Senate a moderately wealthy wholesale grocer and left years later a multimillionaire, was the father-in-law of John D. Rockefeller, Jr. His grandson and namesake, Nelson Aldrich Rockefeller, later became vice president of the United States, and head of the "corporate liberal" wing of the Republican Party.

currency" based on municipal and railroad bonds. But even this bill was defeated.

Meeting setbacks in Congress, the big bankers decided to regroup and turn temporarily to the executive branch. Foreshadowing a later, more elaborate collaboration, two powerful representatives each from the Morgan and Rockefeller banking interests met with Comptroller of the Currency William B. Ridgely in January 1903, to try to persuade him, by administrative fiat, to restrict the volume of loans made by the country banks in the New York money market. The two Morgan men at the meeting were J.P. Morgan and George F. Baker, Morgan's closest friend and associate in the banking business.[26] The two Rockefeller men were Frank Vanderlip and James Stillman, longtime chairman of the board of the National City Bank.[27] The close Rockefeller-Stillman alliance was cemented by the marriage of the two daughters of Stillman to the two sons of William Rockefeller, brother of John D. Rockefeller, Sr., and longtime board member of the National City Bank.[28]

The meeting with the comptroller did not bear fruit, but the lead instead was taken by the secretary of the Treasury himself, Leslie Shaw, formerly presiding officer at the second Indianapolis Monetary Convention, whom President

---

[26] Baker was head of the Morgan-dominated First National Bank of New York, and served as a director of virtually every important Morgan-run enterprise, including: Chase National Bank, Guaranty Trust Company, Morton Trust Company, Mutual Life Insurance Company, AT&T, Consolidated Gas Company of New York, Erie Railroad, New York Central Railroad, Pullman Company, and United States Steel. See Burch, *Elites*, pp. 190, 229.

[27] On the meeting, see Livingston, *Origins*, p. 155.

[28] Burch, *Elites*, pp. 134–35.

Roosevelt appointed to replace Lyman Gage. The unexpected and sudden shift from McKinley to Roosevelt in the presidency meant more than just a turnover of personnel; it meant a fundamental shift from a Rockefeller-dominated to a Morgan-dominated administration. In the same way, the shift from Gage to Shaw was one of the many Rockefeller-to-Morgan displacements.

On monetary and banking matters, however, the Rockefeller and Morgan camps were as one. Secretary Shaw attempted to continue and expand Gage's experiments in trying to make the Treasury function like a central bank, particularly in making open market purchases in recessions, and in using Treasury deposits to bolster the banks and expand the money supply. Shaw violated the statutory institution of the independent Treasury, which had tried to confine government revenues and expenditures to its own coffers. Instead, he expanded the practice of depositing Treasury funds in favored big national banks. Indeed, even banking reformers denounced the deposit of Treasury funds to pet banks as artificially lowering interest rates and leading to artificial expansion of credit. Furthermore, any government deficit would obviously throw a system dependent on a flow of new government revenues into chaos. All in all, the reformers agreed increasingly with the verdict of economist Alexander Purves, that "the uncertainty as to the Secretary's power to control the banks by arbitrary decisions and orders, and the fact that at some future time the country may be unfortunate in its chief Treasury official ... [has] led many to doubt the wisdom" of using the Treasury as a form of central bank.[29] In his last annual report of 1906, Secretary Shaw urged that he be given total power to regulate all the nation's banks. But

---

[29] Livingston, *Origins*, p. 156. See also ibid., pp. 161–62.

the game was up, and by then it was clear to the reformers that Shaw's as well as Gage's proto–central bank manipulations had failed. It was time to undertake a struggle for a fundamental legislative overhaul of the American banking system to bring it under central banking control.[30]

---

[30] On Gage's and Shaw's manipulations, see Rothbard, "Federal Reserve," pp. 94–96; and Milton Friedman and Anna Jacobson Schwartz, *A Monetary History of the United States, 1867–1960* (Princeton, N.J.: National Bureau of Economic Research, 1963), pp. 148–56.

Charles A. Conant, Surplus Capital, and Economic Imperialism

The years shortly before and after 1900 proved to be the beginnings of the drive toward the establishment of a Federal Reserve System. It was also the origin of the gold-exchange standard, the fateful system imposed upon the world by the British in the 1920s and by the United States after World War II at Bretton Woods. Even more than the case of a gold standard *with* a central bank, the gold-exchange standard establishes a system, in the name of gold, which in reality manages to install coordinated international inflationary paper money. The idea was to replace a genuine gold standard, in which each country (or, domestically, each bank) maintains its reserves in gold, by a pseudo-gold standard in which the central bank of the client country maintains its reserves in some key or base currency, say pounds or dollars. Thus, during the 1920s, most countries maintained their reserves in pounds, and only Britain purported to redeem pounds in gold. This meant that these other countries were really on a pound rather than a gold standard, although they were able, at least temporarily, to acquire the prestige of gold. It also meant that when Britain inflated pounds, there was no danger of losing gold to these other countries, who, quite the contrary, happily inflated their own currencies on top of their expanding balances in pounds sterling. Thus, there was generated an unstable, inflationary system—all in the name of gold—in which client states pyramided their own inflation on top of Great Britain's. The system was eventually bound to collapse, as did the gold-exchange standard in the Great Depression and Bretton Woods by the late 1960s. In addition, the close ties based on pounds and then dollars meant that the key or base country was able to exert a form of economic imperialism, joined by its common paper and pseudo-gold inflation, upon the client states using the key money.

By the late 1890s, groups of theoreticians in the United States were working on what would later be called the "Leninist" theory of capitalist imperialism. The theory was originated, not by Lenin but by advocates of imperialism, centering around such Morgan-oriented friends and brain trusters of Theodore Roosevelt as Henry Adams, Brooks Adams, Admiral Alfred T. Mahan, and Massachusetts Senator Henry Cabot Lodge. The idea was that capitalism in the developed countries was "overproducing," not simply in the sense that more purchasing power was needed in recessions, but more deeply in that the rate of profit was therefore inevitably falling. The ever lower rate of profit from the "surplus capital" was in danger of crippling capitalism, except that salvation loomed in the form of foreign markets and especially foreign investments. New and expanded foreign markets would increase profits, at least temporarily, while investments in undeveloped countries would be bound to bring a high rate of profit. Hence, to save advanced capitalism, it was necessary for Western governments to engage in outright imperialist or neo-imperialist ventures, which would force other countries to open their markets for American products and would force open investment opportunities abroad.

Given this doctrine—based on the fallacious Ricardian view that the rate of profit is determined by the stock of capital investment, instead of by the time preferences of everyone in society— there was little for Lenin to change except to give an implicit moral condemnation instead of approval and to emphasize the necessarily temporary nature of the respite imperialism could furnish for capitalists.[31]

Charles Conant set forth the theory of surplus capital in his *A History of Modern Banks of Issue* (1896) and developed it in subsequent essays. The existence of fixed capital and modern technology, Conant claimed, invalidated Say's Law and the concept of equilibrium, and led to chronic "oversavings," which he defined as savings in excess of profitable investment outlets, in the developed Western capitalist world. Business cycles, opined Conant, were inherent in the unregulated activity of modern industrial capitalism. Hence the importance of government-encouraged monopolies and cartels to stabilize markets and the business cycle, and in particular the necessity of economic imperialism to force open profitable outlets abroad for American and other Western surplus capital.

The United States's bold venture into an imperialist war against Spain in 1898 galvanized the energies of Conant and other theoreticians of imperialism. Conant responded with

---

[31] Indeed, the adoption of this theory of the alleged necessity for imperialism in the "later stages" of capitalism went precisely from pro-imperialists like the *U.S. Investor*, Charles A. Conant, and Brooks Adams in 1898–99, read and adopted by the Marxist H. Gaylord Wilshire in 1900–01, in turn read and adopted by the English left-liberal anti-imperialist John A. Hobson, who in turn influenced Lenin. See in particular Norman Etherington, *Theories of Imperialism: War, Conquest, and Capital* (Totowa, N.J.: Barnes and Noble, 1984). See also Etherington, "Reconsidering Theories of Imperialism," *History and Theory* 21, no. 1 (1982): 1–36.

his call for imperialism in "The Economic Basis of Imperialism" in the September 1898 *North American Review*, and in other essays collected in *The United States in the Orient: The Nature of the Economic Problem* and published in 1900. S.J. Chapman, a distinguished British economist, accurately summarized Conant's argument as follows: (1) "In all advanced countries there has been such excessive saving that no profitable investment for capital remains," (2) since all countries do not practice a policy of commercial freedom, "America must be prepared to use force if necessary" to open up profitable investment outlets abroad, and (3) the United States possesses an advantage in the coming struggle, since the organization of many of its industries "in the form of trusts will assist it greatly in the fight for commercial supremacy."[32]

The war successfully won, Conant was particularly enthusiastic about the United States keeping the Philippines, the gateway to the great potential Asian market. The United States, he opined, should not be held back by "an abstract theory" to adopt "extreme conclusions" on applying the doctrines of the Founding Fathers on the importance of the consent of the governed. The Founding Fathers, he declared, surely meant that self-government could only apply to those competent to exercise it, a requirement that clearly did not apply to the backward people of the Philippines. After all, Conant wrote, "Only by the firm hand of the responsible governing races ... can the assurance of uninterrupted progress be conveyed to the tropical and undeveloped countries."[33]

---

[32] Review of Charles A. Conant's *The United States in the Orient*, by S.J. Chapman in *Economic Journal* 2 (1901): 78. See Etherington, *Theories of Imperialism*, p. 24.

[33] David Healy, *U.S. Expansionism: The Imperialist Urge in the 1890s* (Madison: University of Wisconsin Press, 1970), pp. 200–01.

Conant also was bold enough to derive important domestic conclusions from his enthusiasm for imperialism. Domestic society, he claimed, would have to be transformed to make the nation as "efficient" as possible. Efficiency, in particular, meant centralized concentration of power. "Concentration of power, in order to permit prompt and efficient action, will be an almost essential factor in the struggle for world empire." In particular, it was important for the United States to learn from the magnificent centralization of power and purpose in Czarist Russia. The government of the United States would require "a degree of harmony and symmetry which will permit the direction of the whole power of the state toward definite and intelligent policies." The U.S. Constitution would have to be amended to permit a form of czarist absolutism, or at the very least an enormously expanded executive power in foreign affairs.[34]

An interesting case study of business opinion energized and converted by the lure of imperialism was the Boston weekly, the *U.S. Investor*. Before the outbreak of war with Spain in 1898, the *U.S. Investor* denounced the idea of war as a disaster to business. But after the United States launched its war, and Commodore Dewey seized Manila Bay, the *Investor* totally changed its tune. Now it hailed the war as excellent for business, and as bringing about recovery from the previous recession. Soon the *Investor* was happily advocating a policy of "imperialism" to make U.S. prosperity permanent. Imperialism conveyed marvelous benefits to the country. At home, a big army and navy would be valuable in curbing the tendency of democracy to enjoy "a too great freedom from restraint, both of action and of thought." The *Investor* added that "European experience

---

[34] Ibid., pp. 202–03.

demonstrates that the army and navy are admirably adopted to inculcate orderly habits of thought and action."

But an even more important benefit from a policy of permanent imperialism is economic. To keep "capital ... at work," stern necessity requires that "an enlarged field for its product must be discovered." Specifically, "a new field" had to be found for selling the growing flood of goods produced by the advanced nations, and for investment of their savings at profitable rates. The *Investor* exulted in the fact that this new "field lies ready for occupancy. It is to be found among the semi-civilized and barbarian races," in particular the beckoning country of China.

Particularly interesting was the colloquy that ensued between the *Investor*, and the *Springfield (Mass.) Republican*, which still propounded the older theory of free trade and *laissez-faire*. The *Republican* asked why trade with undeveloped countries was not sufficient without burdening U.S. taxpayers with administrative and military overhead. The *Republican* also attacked the new theory of surplus capital, pointing out that only two or three years earlier, businessmen had been loudly calling for more European capital to be invested in American ventures.

To the first charge, the *Investor* fell back on "the experience of the race for, perhaps ninety centuries, [which] has been in the direction of foreign acquisitions as a means of national prosperity." But, more practically, the *Investor* delighted over the goodies that imperialism would bring to American business in the way of government contracts and the governmental development of what would now be called the "infrastructure" of the colonies. Furthermore, as in Britain, a greatly expanded diplomatic service would provide "a new calling for our young men of education and ability."

To the *Republican's* second charge, on surplus capital, the *Investor*, like Conant, developed the idea of a new age that had just arrived in American affairs, an age of large-scale and hence overproduction, an age of a low rate of profit, and consequent formation of trusts in a quest for higher profits through suppression of competition. As the *Investor* put it, "The excess of capital has resulted in an unprofitable competition. To employ Franklin's witticism, the owners of capital are of the opinion they must hang together or else they will all hang separately." But while trusts may solve the problem of specific industries, they did not solve the great problem of a general "congestion of capital." Indeed, wrote the Investor, "finding employment for capital … is now the greatest of all economic problems that confront us."

To the *Investor*, the way out was clear:

> [T]he logical path to be pursued is that of the development of the natural riches of the tropical countries. These countries are now peopled by races incapable on their own initiative of extracting its full riches from their own soil. … This will be attained in some cases by the mere stimulus of government and direction by men of the temperate zones; but it will be attained also by the application of modern machinery and methods of culture to the agricultural and mineral resources of the undeveloped countries.[35]

By the spring of 1901, even the eminent economic theorist John Bates Clark of Columbia University was able to embrace the new creed. Reviewing pro-imperialist works by Conant, Brooks Adams, and the Reverend Josiah Strong in a single

[35] *The Investor*, 19 January 1901, pp. 65–66, cited in Etherington, *Theories of Imperialism*, p. 17. Also ibid., pp. 7–23.

celebratory review in March 1901 in the *Political Science Quarterly*, Clark emphasized the importance of opening foreign markets and particularly of investing American capital "with an even larger and more permanent profit."[36]

J.B. Clark was not the only economist ready to join in apologia for the strong state. Throughout the land by the turn of the twentieth century, a legion of economists and other social scientists had arisen, many of them trained in graduate schools in Germany to learn of the virtues of the inductive method, the German Historical School, and a collectivist, organicist state.

Eager for positions and power commensurate with their graduate training, these new social scientists, in the name of professionalism and technical expertise, prepared to abandon the old *laissez-faire* creed and take their places as apologists and planners in a new, centrally planned state. Professor Edwin R.A. Seligman of Columbia University, of the prominent Wall Street investment banking family of J. and W. Seligman and Company, spoke for many of these social scientists when, in a presidential address before the American Economic Association in 1903, he hailed the "new industrial order."[37] Seligman prophesied that in the new, twentieth century, the possession of economic knowledge would grant economists the power "to control ... and mold" the material forces of progress. As the economist proved able to forecast more accurately, he would

---

[36] Parrini and Sklar, "New Thinking," p. 565, n. 16.

[37] Seligman was also related by marriage to the Loebs and to Paul Warburg of Kuhn, Loeb. Specifically, E.R.A. Seligman's brother, Isaac N., was married to Guta Loeb, sister of Paul Warburg's wife, Nina. See Stephen Birmingham, *Our Crowd: The Jewish Families of New York* (New York: Pocket Books, 1977), app.

be installed as "the real philosopher of social life," and the public would pay "deference to his views."

In his 1899 presidential address, Yale President Arthur Twining Hadley also saw economists developing as society's philosopher-kings. The most important application of economic knowledge, declared Hadley, was leadership in public life, becoming advisers and leaders of national policy. Hadley opined,

> I believe that their [economists'] largest opportunity in the immediate future lies not in theories but in practice, not with students but with statesmen, not in the education of individual citizens, however widespread and salutary, but in the leadership of an organized body politic.[38]

Hadley perceptively saw the executive branch of the government as particularly amenable to access of position and influence to economic advisers and planners. Previously, executives were hampered in seeking such expert counsel by the importance of political parties, their ideological commitments, and their mass base in the voting population. But now, fortunately, the growing municipal reform (soon to be called the Progressive) movement was taking power away from political parties and putting it into the hands of administrators and experts. The "increased centralization of administrative power [was giving] ... the expert a fair chance." And now, on the national scene, the new American leap into imperialism in war against Spain in 1898 galvanized opportunity for increased centralization, executive power, and therefore for administrative and expert planning. Even though Hadley declared himself personally opposed to imperialism,

---

[38] Quoted in Edward T. Silva and Sheila A. Slaughter, *Serving Power: The Making of the Academic Social Science Expert* (Westport, Conn.: Greenwood Press, 1984), p. 103.

he urged economists to leap at this great opportunity for access to power.[39]

The organized economic profession was not slow to grasp this new opportunity. Quickly, the executive and nominating committees of the American Economic Association (AEA) created a five-man special committee to organize and publish a volume on colonial finance. As Silva and Slaughter put it, this new, rapidly put-together volume permitted the AEA to show the power elite

> how the new social science could serve the interests of those who made imperialism a national policy by offering technical solutions to the immediate fiscal problems of colonies as well as providing ideological justifications for acquiring them.[40]

Chairman of the special committee was Professor Jeremiah W. Jenks of Cornell, the major economic adviser to New York Governor Theodore Roosevelt. Another member was Professor E.R.A. Seligman, another key adviser to Roosevelt. A third colleague was Dr. Albert Shaw, influential editor of the *Review of Reviews*, progressive reformer and social scientist, and longtime crony of Roosevelt's. All three were longtime leaders of the American Economic Association. The other two, non-AEA leaders, on the committee were Edward R. Strobel, former assistant secretary of state and adviser to colonial governments, and Charles S. Hamlin, wealthy Boston lawyer and assistant secretary of the Treasury who had long been in the Morgan ambit, and whose wife was a member of the Pruyn family, longtime investors in two Morgan-dominated

---

[39] Ibid., pp. 120–21.

[40] Ibid., p. 133.

concerns: the New York Central Railroad and the Mutual Life Insurance Company of New York.

Essays in Colonial Finance, the volume quickly put together by these five leaders, tried to advise the United States how best to run its newly acquired empire. First, just as the British government insisted when the North American states were its colonies, the colonies should support their imperial government through taxation, whereas control should be tightly exercised by the United States imperial center. Second, the imperial center should build and maintain the economic infrastructure of the colony: canals, railroads, communications. Third, where—as was clearly anticipated—native labor is inefficient or incapable of management, the imperial government should import (white) labor from the imperial center. And, finally, as Silva and Slaughter put it,

> the committee's fiscal recommendations strongly intimated that trained economists were necessary for a successful empire. It was they who must make a thorough study of local conditions to determine the correct fiscal system, gather data, create the appropriate administrative design and perhaps even implement it. In this way, the committee seconded Hadley's views in seeing as an opportunity for economists by identifying a large number of professional positions best filled by themselves.[41]

With the volume written, the AEA cast about for financial support for its publication and distribution. The point was not simply to obtain the financing, but to do so in such a way as to gain the imprimatur of leading members of the power elite on

---

[41] Ibid., p. 135. The volume in question is *Essays in Colonial Finance* (Publications of the American Economic Association, 3rd series, August 1900).

this bold move for power to economists as technocratic expert advisers and administrators in the imperial nation-state.

The American Economic Association found five wealthy businessmen to put up $125, two-fifths of the full cost of publishing *Essays in Colonial Finance*. By compiling the volume and then accepting corporate sponsors, several of whom had an economic stake in the new American empire, the AEA was signaling that the nation's organized economists were (1) wholeheartedly in favor of the new American empire; and (2) willing and eager to play a strong role in advising and administering the empire, a role which they promptly and happily filled, as we shall see in the following section.

In view of the symbolic as well as practical role for the sponsors, a list of the five donors for the colonial finance volume is instructive. One was Isaac N. Seligman, head of the investment banking house of J. and W. Seligman and Company, a company with extensive overseas interests, especially in Latin America. Isaac's brother, E.R.A. Seligman, was a member of the special committee on colonial finance and an author of one of the essays in the volume. Another was William E. Dodge, a partner of the copper mining firm of Phelps, Dodge, and Company and member of a powerful mining family allied to the Morgans. A third donor was Theodore Marburg, an economist who was vice president of the AEA at the time, and also an ardent advocate of imperialism as well as heir to a substantial American Tobacco Company fortune. Fourth was Thomas Shearman, a single-taxer and an attorney for powerful railroad magnate Jay Gould. And last but not least, Stuart Wood, a manufacturer who had a Ph.D. in economics and had been a vice president of the AEA.

Conant, Monetary Imperialism, and the Gold-Exchange Standard

The leap into political imperialism by the United States in the late 1890s was accompanied by economic imperialism, and one key to economic imperialism was monetary imperialism. In brief, the developed Western countries by this time were on the gold standard, while most of the Third World nations were on the silver standard. For the past several decades, the value of silver in relation to gold had been steadily falling, due to (1) an increasing world supply of silver relative to gold, and (2) the subsequent shift of many Western nations from silver or bimetallism to gold, thereby lowering the world's demand for silver as a monetary metal.

The fall of silver value meant monetary depreciation and inflation in the Third World, and it would have been a reasonable policy to shift from a silver-coin to a gold-coin standard. But the new imperialists among U.S. bankers, economists, and politicians were far less interested in the welfare of Third World countries than in foisting a monetary imperialism upon them. For not only would the economies of the imperial center and the client states then be tied together, but they would be tied in such a way that these economies could pyramid their own monetary and bank credit inflation on top of inflation in the United States. Hence, what the new imperialists set out to do was to pressure or coerce Third World countries to adopt, not a genuine gold-coin standard, but a newly conceived "gold-exchange" or dollar standard.

Instead of silver currency fluctuating freely in terms of gold, the silver-gold rate would then be fixed by arbitrary government price-fixing. The silver countries would be silver in name only; a country's monetary reserve would be held, not in silver, but in dollars allegedly redeemable in gold; and these reserves would be held, not in the country itself, but as dollars piled up in New York City. In that way, if U.S. banks inflated their credit, there would be no danger of losing gold abroad, as would happen under a genuine gold standard. For under a true gold standard, no one and no country would be interested in piling up claims to dollars overseas. Instead, they would demand payment of dollar claims in gold. So that even though these American bankers and economists were all too aware, after many decades of experience, of the fallacies and evils of bimetallism, they were willing to impose a form of bimetallism upon client states in order to tie them into U.S. economic imperialism, and to pressure them into inflating their own money supplies on top of dollar reserves supposedly, but not de facto redeemable in gold.

The United States first confronted the problem of silver currencies in a Third World country when it seized control of Puerto Rico from Spain in 1898 and occupied it as a permanent colony. Fortunately for the imperialists, Puerto Rico was already ripe for currency manipulation. Only three years earlier, in 1895, Spain had destroyed the full-bodied Mexican silver currency that its colony had previously enjoyed and replaced it with a heavily debased silver "dollar," worth only 41¢ in U.S. currency. The Spanish government had pocketed the large seigniorage profits from that debasement. The

United States was therefore easily able to substitute its own debased silver dollar, worth only 45.6¢ in gold. Thus, the United States silver currency replaced an even more debased one and also the Puerto Ricans had no tradition of loyalty to a currency only recently imposed by the Spaniards. There was therefore little or no opposition in Puerto Rico to the U.S. monetary takeover.[42]

The major controversial question was what exchange rate the American authorities would fix between the two debased coins: the old Puerto Rican silver peso and the U.S. silver dollar. This was the rate at which the U.S. authorities would compel the Puerto Ricans to exchange their existing coinage for the new American coins. The treasurer in charge of the currency reform for the U.S. government was the prominent Johns Hopkins economist Jacob H. Hollander, who had been special commissioner to revise Puerto Rican tax laws, and who was one of the new breed of academic economists repudiating *laissez-faire* for comprehensive statism. The heavy debtors in Puerto Rico—mainly the large sugar planters— naturally wanted to pay their peso obligations at as cheap a rate as possible; they lobbied for a peso worth 50¢ American. In contrast, the Puerto Rican banker-creditors wanted the rate fixed at 75¢. Since the exchange rate was arbitrary anyway, Hollander and the other American officials decided in the time-honored way of governments: more or less splitting the difference, and fixing a peso equal to 60¢.[43]

---

[42] See the illuminating article by Emily S. Rosenberg, "Foundations of United States International Financial Power: Gold Standard Diplomacy, 1900–1905," *Business History Review* 59 (Summer 1985): 172–73.

[43] Also getting their start in administering imperialism in Puerto Rico were economist and demographer W.H. Willcox of Cornell, who conducted the first census on the island as well as in Cuba in 1900, and

The Philippines, the other Spanish colony grabbed by the United States, posed a far more difficult problem. As in most of the Far East, the Philippines was happily using a perfectly sound silver currency, the Mexican silver dollar. But the United States was anxious for a rapid reform, because its large armed forces establishment suppressing Filipino nationalism required heavy expenses in U.S. dollars, which it of course declared to be legal tender for payments. Since the Mexican silver coin was also legal tender and was cheaper than the U.S. gold dollar, the U.S. military occupation found its revenues being paid in unwanted and cheaper Mexican coins.

Delicacy was required, and in 1901, for the task of currency takeover, the Bureau of Insular Affairs (BIA) of the War Department—the agency running the U.S. occupation of the Philip-pines—hired Charles A. Conant. Secretary of War Elihu Root was a redoubtable Wall Street lawyer in the Morgan ambit who sometimes served as J.P. Morgan's personal attorney. Root took a personal hand in sending Conant to the Philippines. Conant, fresh from the Indianapolis Monetary Commission and before going to New York as a leading investment banker, was, as might be expected, an ardent gold-exchange-standard imperialist as well as the leading theoretician of economic imperialism.

Roland P. Faulkner, statistician and bank reformer first at the University of Pennsylvania, and then head of the Division of Documents at the Library of Congress. Faulkner became commissioner of education in Puerto Rico in 1903, then went on to head the U.S.Commission to Liberia in 1909 and to be a member of the Joint Land Commission of the U.S. and Chinese governments. Harvard economist Thomas S. Adams served as assistant treasurer to Hollander in Puerto Rico. Political scientist William F. Willoughby succeeded Hollander as treasurer (Silva and Slaughter, *Serving Power*, pp. 137–38).

Realizing that the Filipino people loved their silver coins, Conant devised a way to impose a gold U.S. dollar currency upon the country. Under his cunning plan, the Filipinos would continue to have a silver currency; but replacing the full-bodied Mexican silver coin would be an American silver coin tied to gold at a debased value far less than the market exchange value of silver in terms of gold. In this imposed, debased bimetallism, since the silver coin was deliberately overvalued in relation to gold by the U.S. government, Gresham's Law inexorably went into effect. The overvalued silver would keep circulating in the Philippines, and undervalued gold would be kept sharply out of circulation.

The seigniorage profit that the Treasury would reap from the debasement would be happily deposited at a New York bank, which would then function as a "reserve" for the U.S. silver currency in the Philippines. Thus, the New York funds would be used for payment outside the Philippines instead of as coin or specie. Moreover, the U.S. government could issue paper dollars based on its new reserve fund.

It should be noted that Conant originated the gold-exchange scheme as a way of exploiting and controlling Third World economies based on silver. At the same time, Great Britain was introducing similar schemes in its colonial areas in Egypt, in Straits Settlements in Asia, and particularly in India.

Congress, however, pressured by the silver lobby, balked at the BIA's plan. And so the BIA again turned to the seasoned public relations and lobbying skills of Charles A. Conant. Conant swung into action. Meeting with editors of the top financial journals, he secured their promises to write editorials pushing for the Conant plan, many of which he obligingly wrote himself. He was already backed by the American banks of Manila. Recalcitrant U.S. bankers were warned by Conant that they could no longer expect large government deposits from the War Department if they continued to oppose the plan. Furthermore, Conant won the support of the major enemies of his plan, the American silver companies and pro-silver bankers, promising them that if the Philippine currency reform went through, the federal government would buy silver for the new U.S. coinage in the Philippines from these same companies. Finally, the tireless lobbying, and the mixture of bribery and threats by Conant, paid off: Congress passed the Philippine Currency Bill in March 1903.

In the Philippines, however, the United States could not simply duplicate the Puerto Rican example and coerce the conversion of the old for the new silver coinage. The Mexican silver coin was a dominant coin not only in the Far East but throughout the world, and the coerced conversion would have been endless. The U.S. tried; it removed the legal tender privilege from the Mexican coins, and decreed the new U.S. coins be used for taxes, government salaries, and other government payments. But this time the Filipinos happily used the old Mexican coins as money, while the U.S. silver coins disappeared from circulation into payment of taxes and transactions to the United States.

The War Department was beside itself: How could it drive Mexican silver coinage out of the Philippines? In desperation, it turned to the indefatigable Conant, but Conant couldn't join the colonial government in the Philippines because he had just been appointed to a more far-flung presidential commission on international exchange for pressuring Mexico and China to go on a similar gold-exchange standard. Hollander, fresh from his Puerto Rican triumph, was ill. Who else? Conant, Hollander, and several leading bankers told the War Department they could recommend no one for the job, so new then was the profession of technical expertise in monetary imperialism. But there was one more hope, the other pro-cartelist and financial imperialist, Cornell's Jeremiah W. Jenks, a fellow member with Conant of President Roosevelt's new Commission on International Exchange (CIE). Jenks had already paved the way for Conant by visiting English and Dutch colonies in the Far East in 1901 to gain information about running the Philippines. Jenks finally came up with a name, his former graduate student at Cornell, Edwin W. Kemmerer.

Young Kemmerer went to the Philippines from 1903 to 1906 to implement the Conant plan. Based on the theories of Jenks and Conant, and on his own experience in the Philippines, Kemmerer went on to teach at Cornell and then at Princeton, and gained fame throughout the 1920s as the "money doctor," busily imposing the gold-exchange standard on country after country abroad.

Relying on Conant's behind-the-scenes advice, Kemmerer and his associates finally came out with a successful scheme to drive out the Mexican silver coins. It was a plan that relied heavily on government coercion. The United States imposed a legal prohibition on the importation of the Mexican coins, followed by severe taxes on any private Philippine transactions daring to use the Mexican currency. Luckily for the planners, their scheme was aided by a large-scale demand at the time for Mexican silver in northern China, which absorbed silver from the Philippines or that would have been smuggled into the islands. The U.S. success was aided by the fact that the new U.S. silver coins, perceptively called "conants" by the Filipinos, were made up to look very much like the cherished old Mexican coins. By 1905, force, luck, and trickery had prevailed, and the conants (worth 50¢ in U.S. money) were the dominant currency in the Philippines. Soon the U.S. authorities were confident enough to add token copper coins and paper conants as well.[44]

---

[44] See Rosenberg, "Foundations," pp. 177–81. Other economists and social scientists helping to administer imperialism in the Philippines

By 1903, the currency reformers felt emboldened enough to move against the Mexican silver dollar throughout the world. In Mexico itself, U.S. industrialists who wanted to invest there pressured the Mexicans to shift from silver to gold, and they found an ally in Mexico's powerful finance minister, Jose Limantour. But tackling the Mexican silver peso at home would not be an easy task, for the coin was known and used throughout the world, particularly in China, where it formed the bulk of the circulating coinage. Finally, after three-way talks between United States, Mexican, and Chinese officials, the Mexicans and Chinese were induced to send identical notes to the U.S. secretary of state, urging the United States to appoint financial advisers to bring about currency reform and stabilized exchange rates with the gold countries.[45]

These requests gave President Roosevelt, upon securing congressional approval, the excuse to appoint in March 1903

---

were: Carl C. Plehn of the University of California, who served as chief statistician to the Philippine Commission in 1900–01, and Bernard Moses, historian, political scientist, and economist at the University of California, an ardent advocate of imperialism who served on the Philippine Commission from 1901 to 1903, and then became an expert in Latin American affairs, joining in a series of Pan American conferences. Political scientist David P. Barrows became superintendent of schools in Manila and director of education for eight years, from 1901 to 1909. This experience ignited a lifelong interest in the military for Barrows, who, while a professor at Berkeley and a general in the California National Guard in 1934, led the troops that broke the San Francisco longshoremen's strike. During World War II, Barrows carried over his interest in coercion to help in the forced internment of Japanese Americans in concentration camps. On Barrows, see Silva and Slaughter, *Serving Power*, pp. 137–38. On Moses, see Dorfman, *Economic Mind*, pp. 96–98.

[45] Parrini and Sklar, "New Thinking," pp. 573–77; Rosenberg, "Foundations," p. 184.

a three-man Commission on International Exchange to bring about currency reform in Mexico, China, and the rest of the silver-using world. The aim was "to bring about a fixed relationship between the moneys of the gold-standard countries and the present silver-using countries," in order to foster "export trade and investment opportunities" in the gold countries and economic development in the silver countries.

The three members of the CIE were old friends and like-minded colleagues. Chairman was Hugh H. Hanna, of the Indianapolis Monetary Commission; the others were his former chief aide at that commission, Charles A. Conant, and Professor Jeremiah W. Jenks. Conant, as usual, was the major theoretician and finagler. He realized that major opposition to Mexico's and China's going off silver would come from the important Mexican silver industry, and he devised a scheme to get European countries to purchase large amounts of Mexican silver to ease the pain of the shift.

In a trip to European nations in the summer of 1903, however, Conant and the CIE found the Europeans less than enthusiastic about making Mexican silver purchases as well as subsidizing U.S. exports and investments in China, a land whose market they too were coveting. In the United States, on the other hand, major newspapers and financial periodicals, prodded by Conant's public relations work, warmly endorsed the new currency scheme.

In the meanwhile, however, the United States faced similar currency problems in its two new Caribbean protectorates, Cuba and Panama. Panama was easy. The United States occupied the Canal Zone, and would be importing vast amounts of equipment to build the canal, so it decided to impose the American gold dollar as the currency in the nominally independent Republic of Panama. While the gold dollar was the official currency of Panama, the United States imposed as the actual medium of exchange a new debased silver peso worth 50¢. Fortunately, the new peso was almost the same in value as the old Colombian silver coin it forcibly displaced, and so, like Puerto Rico, the takeover could go without a hitch.

Among the U.S. colonies or protectorates, Cuba proved the toughest nut to crack. Despite all of Conant's ministrations, Cuba's currency remained unreformed. Spanish gold and silver coins, French coins, and U.S. currency all circulated side by side, freely fluctuating in response to supply and demand. Furthermore, similar to the pre-reformed Philippines, a fixed bimetallic exchange rate between the cheaper U.S., and the more valuable Spanish and French coins, led the Cubans to return cheaper U.S. coins to the U.S. customs authorities in fees and revenues.

Why then did Conant fail in Cuba? In the first place, strong Cuban nationalism resented U.S. plans for seizing control of their currency. Conant's repeated request in 1903 for a Cuban invitation for the CIE to visit the island met stern rejections from the Cuban government. Moreover, the charismatic U.S. military commander in Cuba, Leonard Wood, wanted to avoid giving the Cubans the impression that plans were afoot to reduce Cuba to colonial status.

The second objection was economic. The powerful sugar industry in Cuba depended on exports to the United States, and a shift from depreciated silver to higher-valued gold money would increase the cost of sugar exports, by an amount Leonard Wood estimated to be about 20 percent. While the same problem had existed for the sugar planters in Puerto Rico, American economic interests, in Puerto Rico and in other countries such as the Philippines, favored forcing formerly silver countries onto a gold-based standard so as to stimulate

U.S. exports into those countries. In Cuba, on the other hand, there was increasing U.S. investment capital pouring into the Cuban sugar plantations, so that powerful and even dominant U.S. economic interests existed on the other side of the currency reform question. Indeed, by World War I, American investments in Cuban sugar reached the sum of $95 million.

Thus, when Charles Conant resumed his pressure for a Cuban gold-exchange standard in 1907, he was strongly opposed by the U.S. governor of Cuba, Charles Magoon, who raised the problem of a gold-based standard crippling the sugar planters. The CIE never managed to visit Cuba, and ironically, Charles Conant died in Cuba, in 1915, trying in vain to convince the Cubans of the virtues of the gold-exchange standard.[46]

The Mexican shift from silver to gold was more gratifying to Conant, but here the reform was effected by Foreign Minister Limantour and his indigenous technicians, with the CIE taking a back seat. However, the success of this shift, in the Mexican Currency Reform Act of 1905, was assured by a world rise in the price of silver, starting the following year, which made gold coins cheaper than silver, with Gresham's Law bringing about a successful gold-coin currency in Mexico. But the U.S. silver coinage in the Philippines ran into trouble because of the rise in the world silver price. Here, the U.S. silver currency in the Philippines was bailed out by coordinated action by the Mexican government, which sold silver in the Philippines to lower the value of silver sufficiently so that the conants could be brought back into circulation.[47]

---

[46] See Rosenberg, "Foundations," pp. 186–88.

[47] It is certainly possible that one of the reasons for the outbreak of the nationalist Mexican Revolution of 1910, in part a revolution against U.S. influence, was reaction against the U.S.-led currency manipulation

The big failure of Conant-CIE monetary imperialism was in China. In 1900, Britain, Japan, and the United States intervened in China to put down the Boxer Rebellion. The three countries thereupon forced defeated China to agree to pay them and all major European powers an indemnity of $333 million. The United States interpreted the treaty as an obligation to pay in gold, but China, on a depreciated silver standard, began to pay in silver in 1903, an action that enraged the three treaty powers. The U.S. minister to China reported that Britain might declare China's payment in silver a violation of the treaty, which would presage military intervention.

Emboldened by United States success in the Philippines, Panama, and Mexico, Secretary of War Root sent Jeremiah W. Jenks on a mission to China in early 1904 to try to transform China from a silver to a gold-exchange standard. Jenks also wrote to President Roosevelt from China urging that the Chinese indemnity to the United States from the Boxer Rebellion be used to fund exchange professorships for 30 years. Jenks's mission, however, was a total failure. The Chinese understood the CIE currency scheme all too well. They saw and denounced the seigniorage of the gold-exchange standard as an irresponsible and immoral debasement of Chinese currency, an act that would impoverish China while adding to the profits of U.S. banks where seigniorage reserve funds would be deposited. Moreover, the Chinese officials saw that shifting the indemnity from silver to gold would enrich the European governments at the expense of the Chinese economy. They also noted that the CIE scheme would establish a foreign controller of the Chinese currency to impose banking regulations and economic reforms on the Chinese economy. We need not

---

and the coerced shift from silver to gold. Certainly, research needs to be done into this possibility.

wonder at the Chinese outrage. China's reaction was its own nationalistic currency reform in 1905, to replace the Mexican silver coin with a new Chinese silver coin, the tael.[48]

Jenks's ignominious failure in China put an end to any formal role for the Commission on International Exchange.[49] An immediately following fiasco blocked the U.S. government's use of economic and financial advisers to spread the gold-exchange standard abroad. In 1905, the State Department hired Jacob Hollander to move another of its Latin American client states, the Dominican Republic, onto the gold-exchange standard. When Hollander accomplished this task by the end of the year, the State Department asked the Dominican government to hire Hollander to work out a plan for financial reform, including a U.S. loan, and a customs service run by the United States to collect taxes for repayment of the loan. Hollander, son-in-law of prominent Baltimore merchant Abraham Hutzler, used his connection with Kuhn, Loeb and Company to place Dominican bonds with that investment bank. Hollander also engaged happily in double-dipping for the same work, collecting fees for the same job from the State Department and from the Dominican government. When this peccadillo was discovered in 1911, the scandal made it impossible for the U.S. government to use its own employees and its own funds to push for gold-exchange experts abroad. From then on, there was more of a public-private partnership between

---

[48] See Rosenberg, "Foundations," pp. 189–92.

[49] The failure, however, did not diminish the U.S. government's demand for Jenks's services. He went on to advise the Mexican government, serve as a member of the Nicaraguan High Commission under President Wilson's occupation regime, and also headed the Far Eastern Bureau of the State Department. See Silva and Slaughter, *Serving Power*, pp. 136–37.

the U.S. government and the investment bankers, with the bankers supplying their own funds, and the State Department supplying good will and more concrete resources.

Thus, in 1911 and 1912, the United States, over great opposition, imposed a gold-exchange standard on Nicaragua. The State Department formally stepped aside but approved Charles Conant's hiring by the powerful investment banking firm of Brown Brothers to bring about a loan and the currency reform. The State Department lent not only its approval to the project, but also its official wires, for Conant and Brown Brothers to conduct the negotiations with the Nicaraguan government.

By the time he died in Cuba in 1915, Charles Conant had made himself the chief theoretician and practitioner of the gold-exchange and the economic imperialist movements. Aside from his successes in the Philippines, Panama, and Mexico, and his failures in Cuba and China, Conant led in pushing for gold-exchange reform and gold-dollar imperialism in Liberia, Bolivia, Guatemala, and Honduras. His magnum opus in favor of the gold-exchange standard, the two-volume *The Principles of Money and Banking* (1905), as well as his pathbreaking success in the Philippines, was followed by a myriad of books, articles, pamphlets, and editorials, always backed up by his personal propaganda efforts.

Particularly interesting were Conant's arguments in favor of a gold-exchange standard, rather than a genuine gold-coin standard. A straight gold-coin standard, Conant believed, did not provide a sufficient amount of gold to provide for the world's monetary needs. Hence, by tying the existing silver standards in the undeveloped countries to gold, the "shortage" of gold could be overcome, and also the economies of the undeveloped countries could be integrated into those of the dominant imperial power. All this could only be done if the gold-exchange standard were "designed and implemented by careful government policy," but of course Conant himself and his friends and disciples always stood ready to advise and provide such implementation.[50]

In addition, adopting a government-managed gold-exchange standard was superior to either genuine gold or bimetallism because it left each state the flexibility of adapting its currency to local needs. As Conant asserted,

> It leaves each state free to choose the means of exchange which conform best to its local conditions. Rich nations are free to choose gold, nations less rich silver, and those whose financial methods are most advanced are free to choose paper.

It is interesting that for Conant, paper was the most "advanced" form of money. It is clear that the devotion to the gold standard of Conant and his colleagues, was only to a debased and inflationary standard, controlled and manipulated by the U.S. government, with gold really serving as a façade of allegedly hard money.

And one of the critical forms of government manipulation and control in Conant's proposed system was the existence and active functioning of a central bank. As a founder of the "science" of financial advising to governments, Conant, followed by his colleagues and disciples, not only pushed a gold-exchange standard wherever he could do so, but also advocated a central bank to manage and control that standard. As Emily Rosenberg points out:

---

[50] Rosenberg, "Foundations," p. 197.

> Conant thus did not neglect ... one of the major revolution-
> ary changes implicit in his system: a new, important role
> for a central bank as a currency stabilizer. Conant strongly
> supported the American banking reform that culminated
> in the Federal Reserve System ... and American financial
> advisers who followed Conant would spread central banking
> systems, along with gold-standard currency reforms, to the
> countries they advised.[51]

Along with a managed gold-exchange standard would come,
as replacement for the old free-trade, nonmanaged, gold-coin
standard, a world of imperial currency blocs, which "would
necessarily come into being as lesser countries deposited
their gold stabilization funds in the banking systems of more
advanced countries."[52] New York and London banks, in particular, shaped up as the major reserve fund-holders in the
developing new world monetary order.

It is no accident that the United States' major financial and
imperial rival, Great Britain, which was pioneering in imposing gold-exchange standards in its own colonial area at this
time, built upon this experience to impose a gold-exchange
standard, marked by all European currencies pyramiding on
top of British inflation, during the 1920s. That disastrous inflationary experiment led straight to the worldwide banking crash
and the general shift to fiat paper moneys in the early 1930s.
After World War II, the United States took up the torch of
a world gold-exchange standard at Bretton Woods, with the
dollar replacing the pound sterling in a worldwide inflationary
system that lasted approximately 25 years.

---

[51] Ibid., p. 198.

[52] Ibid.

Nor should it be thought that Charles A. Conant was the purely disinterested scientist he claimed to be. His currency reforms directly benefited his investment banker employers.

Thus, Conant was treasurer, from 1902 to 1906, of the Morgan-run Morton Trust Company of New York, and it was surely no coincidence that Morton Trust was the bank that held the reserve funds for the governments of the Philippines, Panama, and the Dominican Republic, after their respective currency reforms. In the Nicaragua negotiations, Conant was employed by the investment bank of Brown Brothers, and in pressuring other countries he was working for Speyer and Company and other investment bankers.

After Conant died in 1915, there were few to pick up the mantle of foreign financial advising. Hollander was in disgrace after the Dominican debacle. Jenks was aging, and lived in the shadow of his China failure, but the State Department did appoint Jenks to serve as a director of the Nicaraguan National Bank in 1917, and also hired him to study the Nicaraguan financial picture in 1925.

But the true successor of Conant was Edwin W. Kemmerer, the "money doctor." After his Philippine experience, Kemmerer joined his old Professor Jenks at Cornell, and then moved to Princeton in 1912, publishing his book *Modern Currency Reforms* in 1916. As the leading foreign financial adviser of the 1920s, Kemmerer not only imposed central banks and a gold-exchange standard on Third World countries, but he also got them to levy higher taxes. Kemmerer, too, combined his public employment with service to leading international bankers. During the 1920s, Kemmerer worked as banking expert for the U.S. government's Dawes Commission, headed special financial advisory missions to more than a dozen countries, and was kept on a handsome retainer by the distinguished investment banking firm of Dillon, Read from 1922 to 1929. In that era, Kemmerer and his mentor Jenks were the only foreign currency reform experts available for advising. In the late 1920s, Kemmerer helped establish a chair of international economics at Princeton, which he occupied, and from which he could train students like Arthur N. Young and William W. Cumberland. In the mid-1920s, the money doctor served as president of the American Economic Association.[53]

---

[53] For an excellent study of the Kemmerer missions in the 1920s, see Robert N. Seidel, "American Reformers Abroad: The Kemmerer Missions in South America, 1932–1931," *Journal of Economic History* 32 (June 1972): 520–45.

Jacob Schiff Ignites the Drive for a Central Bank

The defeat of the Fowler Bill for a broader asset currency and branch banking in 1902, coupled with the failure of Treasury Secretary Shaw's attempts of 1903–1905 to use the Treasury as a central bank, led the big bankers and their economist allies to adopt a new solution: the frank imposition of a central bank in the United States.

The campaign for a central bank was kicked off by a fateful speech in January 1906 by the powerful Jacob H. Schiff, head of the Wall Street investment bank of Kuhn, Loeb and Company, before the New York Chamber of Commerce. Schiff complained that in the autumn of 1905, when "the country needed money," the Treasury, instead of working to expand the money supply, reduced government deposits in the national banks, thereby precipitating a financial crisis, a "disgrace" in which the New York clearinghouse banks had been forced to contract their loans drastically, sending interest rates sky-high. An "elastic currency" for the nation was therefore imperative, and Schiff urged the New York chamber's committee on finance to draw up a comprehensive plan for a modern banking system to provide for an elastic currency.[54] A colleague who had already been agitating for a central bank behind the scenes was Schiff's partner, Paul Moritz Warburg, who had suggested the plan to Schiff as early as 1903. Warburg had emigrated from the German investment firm of M.M. Warburg and Company in 1897, and before long his major function at Kuhn, Loeb was to agitate to bring the blessings of European central banking to the United States.[55]

It took less than a month for the finance committee of the New York chamber to issue its report, but the bank reformers were furious, denouncing it as remarkably ignorant. When Frank A. Vanderlip, of Rockefeller's flagship bank, the National City Bank of New York, reported on this development, his boss, James Stillman, suggested that a new five-man special commission be set up by the New York chamber to come back with a plan for currency reform.

In response, Vanderlip proposed that the five-man commission consist of himself; Schiff; J.P. Morgan; George Baker of the First National Bank of New York, Morgan's closest and longest associate; and former Secretary of the Treasury Lyman Gage, now president of the Rockefeller-controlled U.S. Trust Company. Thus, the commission would consist of two Rockefeller men

---

[54] On Schiff's speech, see *Bankers Magazine* 72 (January 1906): 114–15.

[55] Schiff and Warburg were related by marriage. Schiff, from a prominent German banker family himself, was a son-in-law of Solomon Loeb, cofounder of Kuhn, Loeb; and Warburg, husband of Nina Loeb, was another son-in-law of Solomon Loeb's by a second wife. The incestuous circle was completed when Schiff's daughter Frieda married Paul Warburg's brother Felix, another partner of Schiff's and Paul Warburg's. See Birmingham, *Our Crowd*, pp. 21, 209–10, 383, and appendix. See also Jacques Attali, *A Man of Influence: Sir Siegmund Warburg, 1902–82* (London: Weidenfeld and Nicholson, 1986), p. 53.

(Vanderlip and Gage), two Morgan men (Morgan and Baker), and one representative from Kuhn, Loeb. Only Vanderlip was available to serve, however, so the commission had to be redrawn. In addition to Vanderlip, beginning in March 1906, there sat, instead of Schiff, his close friend Isidore Straus, a director of R.H. Macy and Company. Instead of Morgan and Baker there now served two Morgan men: Dumont Clarke, president of the American Exchange National Bank and a personal adviser to J.P. Morgan, and Charles A. Conant, treasurer of Morton and Company. The fifth man was a veteran of the Indianapolis Monetary Convention, John Claflin, of H.B. Claflin and Company, a large integrated wholesaling concern. Coming on board as secretary of the new currency committee was Vanderlip's old friend Joseph French Johnson, now of New York University, who had been calling for a central bank since 1900.

The commission used the old Indianapolis questionnaire technique: acquiring legitimacy by sending out a detailed questionnaire on currency to a number of financial leaders. With Johnson in charge of mailing and collating the questionnaire replies, Conant spent his time visiting and interviewing the heads of the central banks in Europe.

The special commission delivered its report to the New York Chamber of Commerce in October 1906. To eliminate instability and the danger of an inelastic currency, the commission called for the creation of a "central bank of issue under the control of the government." In keeping with other bank reformers, such as Professor Abram Piatt Andrew of Harvard University, Thomas Nixon Carver of Harvard, and Albert Strauss, partner of J.P. Morgan and Company, the commission was scornful of Secretary Shaw's attempt to use the Treasury as central bank. Shaw was particularly obnoxious because he was still insisting, in his last annual report of 1906, that the Treasury, under his aegis, had constituted a "great central bank." The commission, along with the other reformers, denounced the Treasury for overinflating by keeping interest rates excessively low; a central bank, in contrast, would have much larger capital and undisputed control over the money market, and thus would be able to manipulate the discount rate effectively to keep the economy under proper control. The important point, declared the committee, is that there be "centralization of financial responsibility." In the meantime, short of establishing a central bank, the committee urged that, at the least, the national banks' powers to issue notes should be expanded to include being based on general assets as well as government bonds.[56]

After drafting and publishing this "Currency Report," the reformers used the report as the lever for expanding the agitation for a central bank and broader note-issue powers to other corporate and financial institutions. The next step was the powerful American Bankers Association (ABA). In 1905, the executive council of the ABA had appointed a currency committee which, the following year, recommended an emergency assets currency that would be issued by a federal commission, resembling an embryonic central bank. In a tumultuous plenary session of the ABA convention in October 1906, the ABA rejected this plan, but agreed to appoint a 15-man currency commission that was instructed to meet with the New York chamber's currency committee and attempt to agree on appropriate legislation.

Particularly prominent on the ABA currency commission were:

- Arthur Reynolds, president of the Des Moines National Bank, close to the Morgan-oriented Des Moines Regency, and brother of the prominent Chicago banker, George M. Reynolds, formerly of Des Moines and then president of

---

[56] See Livingston, *Origins*, pp. 159–64.

the Morgan-oriented Continental National Bank of Chicago and the powerful chairman of the executive council of the ABA;

- James B. Forgan, president of the Rockefeller-run First National Bank of Chicago, and close friend of Jacob Schiff of Kuhn, Loeb, as well as of Vanderlip;

- Joseph T. Talbert, vice president of the Rockefeller-dominated Commercial National Bank of Chicago, and soon to become vice president of Rockefeller's flagship bank, the National City Bank of New York;

- Myron T. Herrick, one of the most prominent Rockefeller politicians and businessmen in the country. Herrick was the head of the Cleveland Society of Savings, and was part of the small team of close Rockefeller business allies who, along with Mark Hanna, bailed out Governor William McKinley from bankruptcy in 1893. Herrick was a previous president of the ABA, had just finished a two-year stint as governor of Ohio, and was later to become ambassador to France under his old friend and political ally William Howard Taft as well as later under President Warren G. Harding, and a recipient of Herrick's political support and financial largesse; and

- Chairman of the ABA commission, A. Barton Hepburn, president of one of the leading Morgan commercial banks, the Chase National Bank of New York, and author of the well-regarded *History of Coinage and Currency in the United States*.

After meeting with Vanderlip and Conant as the representatives from the New York Chamber of Commerce committee, the ABA commission, along with Vanderlip and Conant, agreed on at least the transition demands of the reformers. The ABA commission presented proposals to the public, the press, and the Congress in December 1906 for a broader asset currency as well as provisions for emergency issue of bank notes by national banks.

But just as sentiment for a broader asset currency became prominent, the bank reformers began to worry about an uncontrolled adoption of such a currency. For that would mean that national bank credit and notes would expand, and that, in the existing system, small state banks would be able to pyramid and inflate credit on top of the national credit, using the expanded national bank notes as their reserves. The reformers wanted a credit inflation controlled by and confined to the large national banks; they most emphatically did not want uncontrolled state bank inflation that would siphon resources to small entrepreneurs and "speculative" marginal producers. The problem was aggravated by the accelerated rate of increase in the number of small Southern and Western state banks after 1900. Another grave problem for the reformers was that commercial paper was a different system from that of Europe. In Europe, commercial paper, and hence bank assets, were two-name notes endorsed by a small group of wealthy acceptance banks. In contrast to this acceptance paper system, commercial paper in the United States was unendorsed single-name paper, with the bank taking a chance on the creditworthiness of the business borrower. Hence, a decentralized financial system in the United States was not subject to big-banker control.

Worries about the existing system and hence about uncontrolled asset currency were voiced by the top bank reformers. Thus, Vanderlip expressed concern that "there are so many state banks that might count these [national bank] notes in their reserves." Schiff warned that "it would prove unwise, if not dangerous, to clothe six thousand banks or more with the privilege to issue independently a purely credit currency." And, from the Morgan side, a similar concern was voiced by

Victor Morawetz, the powerful chairman of the board of the Atchison, Topeka and Santa Fe Railroad.[57]

Taking the lead in approaching this problem of small banks and decentralization was Paul Moritz Warburg, of Kuhn, Loeb, fresh from his banking experience in Europe. In January 1907, Warburg began what would become years of tireless agitation for central banking with two articles: "Defects and Needs of our Banking System" and "A Plan for a Modified Central Bank."[58] Calling openly for a central bank, Warburg pointed out that one of the important functions of such a bank would be to restrict the eligibility of bank assets to be used for expansion of bank deposits. Presumably, too, the central bank could move to require banks to use acceptance paper or otherwise try to create an acceptance market in the United States.[59]

---

[57] Livingston, *Origins*, pp. 168–69.

[58] See the collection of Warburg's essays in Paul M. Warburg, *The Federal Reserve System*, 2 vols. (New York: Macmillan, 1930). See also Warburg, "Essays on Banking Reform in the United States," *Proceedings of the Academy of Political Science* 4 (July 1914): 387–612.

[59] When the Federal Reserve System was established, Warburg boasted of his crucial role in persuading the Fed to create an acceptance market in the U.S. by agreeing to purchase all acceptance paper available from a few large acceptance banks at subsidized rates. In that way, the Fed provided an unchecked channel for inflationary credit expansion. The acceptance program helped pave the way for the 1929 crash.

It was surely no accident that Warburg himself was the principal beneficiary of this policy. Warburg became chairman of the board, from its founding in 1920, of the International Acceptance Bank, the world's largest acceptance bank, as well as director of the Westinghouse Acceptance Bank and of several other acceptance houses. In 1919, Warburg was the chief founder and chairman of the executive committee of the American Acceptance Council, the trade association of acceptance

By the summer of 1907, *Bankers Magazine* was reporting a decline in influential banker support for broadening asset currency and a strong move toward the "central bank project." *Bankers Magazine* noted as a crucial reason the fact that asset currency would be expanding bank services to "small producers and dealers."[60]

---

houses. See Murray N. Rothbard, *America's Great Depression*, 4th ed. (New York: Richardson and Snyder, 1983), pp. 119–23.

[60] *Bankers Magazine* 75 (September 1907): 314–15.

The Panic of 1907 and Mobilization for a Central Bank

A severe financial crisis, the panic of 1907, struck in early October. Not only was there a general recession and contraction, but the major banks in New York and Chicago were, as in most other depressions in American history, allowed by the government to suspend specie payments, that is, to continue in operation while being relieved of their contractual obligation to redeem their notes and deposits in cash or in gold. While the Treasury had stimulated inflation during 1905–1907, there was nothing it could do to prevent suspensions of payment, or to alleviate "the competitive hoarding of currency" after the panic, that is, the attempt to demand cash in return for increasingly shaky bank notes and deposits.

Very quickly after the panic, banker and business opinion consolidated on behalf of a central bank, an institution that could regulate the economy and serve as a lender of last resort to bail banks out of trouble. The reformers now faced a twofold task: hammering out details of a new central bank, and more important, mobilizing public opinion on its behalf. The first step in such mobilization was to win the support of the nation's academics and experts. The task was made easier by the growing alliance and symbiosis between academia and the power elite.

Two organizations that proved particularly useful for this mobilization were the American Academy of Political and Social
Science (AAPSS) of Philadelphia, and the Academy of Political
Science (APS) of Columbia University, both of which included
in their ranks leading corporate liberal businessmen, financiers,
attorneys, and academics. Nicholas Murray Butler, the highly
influential president of Columbia University, explained that the
Academy of Political Science "is an intermediary between ...
the scholars and the men of affairs, those who may perhaps be
said to be amateurs in scholarship." Here, he pointed out, was
where they "come together."[61]

It is not surprising, then, that the American Academy of
Political and Social Science, the American Association for
the Advancement of Science, and Columbia University held
three symposia during the winter of 1907–1908, each calling
for a central bank, and thereby disseminating the message of
a central bank to a carefully selected elite public. Not surprising, too, was that E.R.A. Seligman was the organizer of the
Columbia conference, gratified that his university was providing a platform for leading bankers and financial journalists to
advocate a central bank, especially, he noted, because "it is
proverbially difficult in a democracy to secure a hearing for
the conclusions of experts." Then in 1908 Seligman collected
the addresses into a volume, *The Currency Problem*.

Professor Seligman set the tone for the Columbia gathering in his opening address. The panic of 1907, he alleged,
was moderate because its effects had been tempered by the
growth of industrial trusts, which provided a more controlled
and "more correct adjustment of present investment to future
needs" than would a "horde of small competitors." In that way,
Seligman displayed no comprehension of how competitive

---

[61] Livingston, *Origins*, p. 175, n. 30.

markets facilitate adjustments. One big problem, however, still remained for Seligman. The horde of small competitors, for whom Seligman had so much contempt, still prevailed in the field of currency and banking. The problem was that the banking system was still decentralized. As Seligman declared,

> Even more important than the inelasticity of our note issue is its decentralization. The struggle which has been victoriously fought out everywhere else [in creating trusts] must be undertaken here in earnest and with vigor.[62]

The next address was that of Frank Vanderlip. To Vanderlip, in contrast to Seligman, the panic of 1907 was "one of the great calamities of history"—the result of a decentralized, competitive American banking system, with 15,000 banks all competing vigorously for control of cash reserves. The terrible thing is that "each institution stands alone, concerned first with its own safety, and using every endeavor to pile up reserves without regard" to the effect of such actions on other banking institutions. This backward system had to be changed, to follow the lead of other great nations, where a central bank is able to mobilize and centralize reserves, and create an elastic currency system. Putting the situation in virtually Marxian terms, Vanderlip declared that the alien external power of the free and competitive market must be replaced by central control following modern, allegedly scientific principles of banking.

Thomas Wheelock, editor of the *Wall Street Journal*, then rung the changes on the common theme by applying it to the volatile call loan market in New York. The market is volatile, Wheelock claimed, because the small country banks are able to lend on that market, and their deposits in New York banks

---

[62] Ibid., p. 177.

then rise and fall in uncontrolled fashion. Therefore, there must be central corporate control over country bank money in the call loan market.

A. Barton Hepburn, head of Morgan's Chase National Bank, came next, and spoke of the great importance of having a central bank that would issue a monopoly of bank notes. It was particularly important that the central bank be able to discount the assets of national banks, and thus supply an elastic currency.

The last speaker was Paul Warburg, who lectured his audience on the superiority of European over American banking, particularly in (1) having a central bank, as against decentralized American banking, and (2)—his old hobby horse—enjoying "modern" acceptance paper instead of single-name promissory notes. Warburg emphasized that these two institutions must function together. In particular, tight government central bank control must replace competition and decentralization: "Small banks constitute a danger."

The other two symposia were very similar. At the AAPSS symposium in Philadelphia, in December 1907, several leading investment bankers and Comptroller of the Currency William B. Ridgely came out in favor of a central bank. It was no accident that members of the AAPSS's advisory committee on currency included A. Barton Hepburn; Morgan attorney and statesman Elihu Root; Morgan's longtime personal attorney, Francis Lynde Stetson; and J.P. Morgan himself. Meanwhile the AAAS symposium in January 1908 was organized by none other than Charles A. Conant, who happened to be chairman of the AAAS's social and economic section for the year. Speakers included Columbia economist J.B. Clark, Frank Vanderlip, Conant, and Vanderlip's friend George E. Roberts, head of the Rockefeller-oriented Commercial National Bank of Chicago, who would later wind up at the National City Bank.

All in all, the task of the bank reformers was well summed up by J.R. Duffield, secretary of the Bankers Publishing Company, in January 1908: "It is recognized generally that before legislation can be had there must be an educational campaign carried on, first among the bankers, and later among commercial organizations, and finally among the people as a whole." That strategy was well under way.

During the same month, the legislative lead in banking reform was taken by the formidable Senator Nelson W. Aldrich (R-R.I.), head of the Senate Finance Committee, and, as the father-in-law of John D. Rockefeller, Jr., Rockefeller's man in the U.S. Senate. He introduced the Aldrich Bill, which focused on a relatively minor interbank dispute about whether and on what basis the national banks could issue special emergency currency. A compromise was finally hammered out and passed, as the Aldrich-Vreeland Act, in 1908.[63] But the important part of the Aldrich-Vreeland Act, which got very little public attention, but was perceptively hailed by the bank reformers, was the establishment of a National Monetary Commission that would investigate the currency question and suggest proposals for comprehensive banking reform. Two enthusiastic comments on the monetary commission were particularly perceptive and prophetic. One was that of Sereno S. Pratt of the *Wall Street Journal*. Pratt virtually conceded that the purpose of the commission was to swamp the public with supposed expertise and thereby "educate" them into supporting banking reform:

---

[63] The emergency currency provision was only used once, shortly before the provision expired, in 1914, and after the establishment of the Federal Reserve System.

Reform can only be brought about by educating the people
up to it, and such education must necessarily take much
time. In no other way can such education be effected more
thoroughly and rapidly than by means of a commission …
[that] would make an international study of the subject and
present an exhaustive report, which could be made the basis
for an intelligent agitation.

The results of the "study" were of course predetermined,
as would be the membership of the allegedly impartial
study commission.

Another function of the commission, as stated by Festus
J. Wade, St. Louis banker and member of the currency commission of the American Bankers Association, was to "keep
the financial issue out of politics" and put it squarely in
the safe custody of carefully selected "experts."[64] Thus, the
National Monetary Commission (NMC) was the apotheosis
of the clever commission concept, launched in Indianapolis
a decade earlier.

Aldrich lost no time setting up the NMC, which was
launched in June 1908. The official members were an equal
number of senators and representatives, but these were mere
window dressing. The real work would be done by the copi-
ous staff, appointed and directed by Aldrich, who told his
counterpart in the House, Cleveland Republican Theodore
Burton: "My idea is, of course, that everything shall be done
in the most quiet manner possible, and without any public
announcement." From the beginning, Aldrich determined that
the NMC would be run as an alliance of Rockefeller, Morgan,
and Kuhn, Loeb people. The two top expert posts advising
or joining the commission were both suggested by Morgan

---

[64] Livingston, *Origins*, pp. 182–83.

leaders. On the advice of J.P. Morgan, seconded by Jacob Schiff, Aldrich picked as his top adviser the formidable Henry P. Davison, Morgan partner, founder of Morgan's Bankers Trust Company, and vice president of George F. Baker's First National Bank of New York. It would be Davison who, on the outbreak of World War I, would rush to England to cement J.P. Morgan and Company's close ties with the Bank of England, and to receive an appointment as monopoly underwriter for all British and French government bonds to be floated in the United States for the duration of the war. For technical economic expertise, Aldrich accepted the recommendation of President Roosevelt's close friend and fellow Morgan man, Charles Eliot, president of Harvard University, who urged the appointment of Harvard economist A. Piatt Andrew. And an ex officio commission member chosen by Aldrich himself was George M. Reynolds, president of the Rockefeller-oriented Continental National Bank of Chicago.

The NMC spent the fall touring Europe and conferring on information and strategy with heads of large European banks and central banks. As director of research, A. Piatt Andrew began to organize American banking experts and to commission reports and studies. The National City Bank's foreign exchange department was commissioned to write papers on bankers' acceptances and foreign debt, while Warburg and Bankers Trust official Fred Kent wrote on the European discount market.

Having gathered information and advice in Europe in the fall of 1908, the NMC was ready to go into high gear by the end of the year. In December, the commission hired the inevitable Charles A. Conant for research, public relations, and agitprop. Behind the façade of the congressmen and senators on the commission, Senator Aldrich began to form and expand his inner circle, which soon included Warburg and Vanderlip. Warburg formed around him a subcircle of friends and acquaintances from the currency committee of the New York Merchants' Association, headed by Irving T. Bush, and from the top ranks of the American Economic Association, to whom he had delivered an address advocating central banking in December 1908. Warburg met and corresponded frequently with leading academic economists advocating banking reform, including E.R.A. Seligman; Thomas Nixon Carver of Harvard; Henry R. Seager of Columbia; Davis R. Dewey, historian of banking at MIT, longtime secretary-treasurer of the AEA and brother of the progressive philosopher John Dewey; Oliver M.W. Sprague, professor of banking at Harvard, of the Morgan-connected Sprague family; Frank W. Taussig of Harvard; and Irving Fisher of Yale.

During 1909, however, the reformers faced an important problem: they had to bring such leading bankers as James B. Forgan, head of the Rockefeller-oriented First National Bank of Chicago, solidly into line in support of a central bank. It was not that Forgan objected to centralized reserves or a lender of last resort—quite the contrary. It was rather that Forgan recognized that, under the national banking system, large banks such as his own were already performing quasi-central banking functions with their own country bank depositors; and he didn't want his bank deprived of such functions by a new central bank.

The bank reformers therefore went out of their way to bring such men as Forgan into enthusiastic support for the new scheme. In his presidential address to the powerful American Bankers Association in mid-September 1909, George M. Reynolds not only came out flatly in favor of a central bank in America, to be modeled after the German Reichsbank; he also assured Forgan and others that such a central bank would act as depository of reserves only for the large national banks in the central reserve cities, while the national banks would continue to hold deposits for the country banks. Mollified, Forgan held a private conference with Aldrich's inner circle and came fully on board for the central bank. As an outgrowth of Forgan's concerns, the reformers decided to cloak their new central bank in a spurious veil of "regionalism" and "decentralism" through establishing regional reserve centers, that would provide the appearance of virtually independent regional central banks to cover the reality of an orthodox European central bank monolith. As a result, noted railroad attorney Victor Morawetz made his famous speech in November 1909, calling for regional banking districts under the ultimate direction of one central control board. Thus, reserves and note issue would be supposedly decentralized in the hands of the regional reserve banks, while they would really be centralized and coordinated by the central control board. This, of course, was the scheme eventually adopted in the Federal Reserve System.[65]

On September 14, at the same time as Reynolds's address to the nation's bankers, another significant address took place. President William Howard Taft, speaking in Boston, suggested that the country seriously consider establishing a central bank. Taft had been close to the reformers—especially his Rockefeller-oriented friends Aldrich and Burton—since

---

[65] Victor Morawetz was an eminent attorney in the Morgan ambit who served as chairman of the executive committee of the Morgan-run Atchison, Topeka and Santa Fe Railway, and member of the board of the Morgan-dominated National Bank of Commerce. In 1908, Morawetz, along with J.P. Morgan's personal attorney, Francis Lynde Stetson, had been the principal drafter of an unsuccessful Morgan-National Civic Federation bill for a federal incorporation law to regulate and cartelize American corporations. Later, Morawetz was to be a top consultant to another "progressive" reformer of Woodrow Wilson's, the Federal Trade Commission. On Morawetz, see Rothbard, "Federal Reserve," p. 99.

1900. But the business press understood the great significance of this public address, that it was, as the *Wall Street
Journal* put it, a crucial step "toward removing the subject
from the realm of theory to that of practical politics."[66]

One week later, a fateful event in American history occurred.
The banking reformers moved to escalate their agitation by
creating a virtual government-bank-press complex to drive
through a central bank. On September 22, 1909, the *Wall
Street Journal* took the lead in this development by beginning a notable, front-page, 14-part series on "A Central Bank
of Issue." These were unsigned editorials by the *Journal*,
but they were actually written by the ubiquitous Charles A.
Conant, from his vantage point as salaried chief propagandist
of the U.S. government's National Monetary Commission.
The series was a summary of the reformers' position, also
going out of the way to assure the Forgans of this world that
the new central bank "would probably deal directly only with
the larger national banks, leaving it for the latter to rediscount
for their more remote correspondents."[67] To the standard arguments for a central bank—"elasticity" of the money supply,
protecting bank reserves by manipulating the discount rate
and the international flow of gold, and combating crisis by
bailing out individual banks—Conant added a Conant twist:
the importance of regulating interest rates and the flow of
capital in a world marked by surplus capital. Government debt
would, for Conant, provide the important function of sopping
up surplus capital; that is, providing profitable outlets for savings by financing government expenditures.

---

[66] *Wall Street Journal*, 16 September 1909, p. 1. Cited in Livingston,
Origins, p. 191.

[67] Ibid.

The *Wall Street Journal* series inaugurated a shrewd and successful campaign by Conant to manipulate the nation's press and get it behind the idea of a central bank. Building on his experience in 1898, Conant, along with Aldrich's secretary, Arthur B. Shelton, prepared abstracts of commission materials for the newspapers during February and March of 1910. Soon Shelton recruited J.P. Gavitt, head of the Washington bureau of the Associated Press, to scan commission abstracts, articles, and forthcoming books for "newsy paragraphs" to catch the eye of newspaper editors.

The academic organizations proved particularly helpful to the NMC, lending their cloak of disinterested expertise to the endeavor. In February, Robert E. Ely, secretary of the APS, proposed to Aldrich that a special volume of its *Proceedings* be devoted to banking and currency reform, to be published in cooperation with the NMC, in order to "popularize in the best sense, some of the valuable work of [the] Commission."[68] And yet, Ely had the gall to add that, even though the APS would advertise the NMC's arguments and conclusions, it would retain its "objectivity" by avoiding its own specific policy recommendations. As Ely put it, "We shall not advocate a central bank, but we shall only give the best results of your work in condensed form and untechnical language."

The AAPSS, too, weighed in with its own special volume, *Banking Problems* (1910), featuring an introduction by A. Piatt Andrew of Harvard and the NMC and articles by veteran bank reformers such as Joseph French Johnson, Horace White, and Morgan Bankers Trust official Fred I. Kent. But most of the articles were from leaders of Rockefeller's National City Bank of New York, including George E. Roberts, a former Chicago banker and U.S. Mint official about to join National City.

---

[68] Ibid., p. 194.

Meanwhile, Paul M. Warburg capped his lengthy campaign for a central bank in a famous speech to the New York YMCA on March 23, on "A United Reserve Bank for the United States." Warburg basically outlined the structure of his beloved German Reichsbank, but he was careful to begin his talk by noting a recent poll in the *Banking Law Journal* that 60 percent of the nation's bankers favored a central bank provided it was "not controlled by 'Wall Street or any monopolistic interest.'" To calm this fear, Warburg insisted that, semantically, the new reserve bank *not* be called a central bank, and that the reserve bank's governing board be chosen by government officials, merchants and bankers—with bankers, of course, dominating the choices. He also provided a distinctive Warburg twist by insisting that the reserve bank replace the hated single-name paper system of commercial credit dominant in the United States by the European system whereby a reserve bank provided a guaranteed and subsidized market for two-named commercial paper endorsed by acceptance banks. In this way, the united reserve bank would correct the "complete lack of modern bills of exchange" (that is, acceptances) in the United States. Warburg added that the entire idea of a free and self-regulating market was obsolete, particularly in the money market. Instead, the action of the market must be replaced by "the best judgment of the best experts." And guess *who* was slated to be one of the best of those best experts?

The greatest cheerleader for the Warburg plan, and the man who introduced the APS's *Reform of the Currency* (1911), the volume on banking reform featuring Warburg's speech, was

Warburg's kinsman and member of the Seligman investment banking family, Columbia economist E.R.A. Seligman.[69]

So delighted was the Merchants' Association of New York with Warburg's speech that it distributed 30,000 copies during the spring of 1910. Warburg had paved the way for this support by regularly meeting with the currency committee of the Merchants' Assocation since October 1908, and his efforts were aided by the fact that the resident expert for that committee was none other than Joseph French Johnson.

At the same time, in the spring of 1910, the numerous research volumes published by the NMC poured onto the market. The object was to swamp public opinion with a parade of impressive analytic and historical scholarship, all allegedly "scientific" and "value-free," but all designed to aid in furthering the common agenda of a central bank. Typical was E.W. Kemmerer's mammoth statistical study of seasonal variations in the demand for money. Stress was laid on the problem of the "inelasticity" of the supply of cash, in particular the difficulty of expanding that supply when needed. While Kemmerer felt precluded from spelling out the policy implications—establishing a central bank—in the book, his acknowledgments in the preface to Fred Kent and the inevitable Charles Conant were a tip-off to the cognoscenti, and Kemmerer himself disclosed them in his address to the Academy of Political Science the following November.

Now that the theoretical and scholarly groundwork had been laid, by the latter half of 1910, it was time to formulate a concrete practical plan and put on a mighty *putsch* on its behalf. In *Reform of the Currency*, published by the APS, Warburg

---

[69] See Rothbard, "Federal Reserve," pp. 98–99. Also, on Warburg's speech, see Livingston, *Origins*, pp. 194–98.

made the point with crystal clarity: "Advance is possible only by outlining a tangible plan" that would set the terms of the debate from then on.[70]

The tangible plan phase of the central bank movement was launched by the ever pliant APS, which held a monetary conference in November 1910, in conjunction with the New York Chamber of Commerce and the Merchants' Association of New York. The members of the NMC were the guests of honor at this conclave, and delegates were chosen by governors of 22 states, as well as presidents of 24 chambers of commerce. Also attending were a large number of economists, monetary analysts, and representatives of most of the top banks in the country. Attendants at the conference included Frank Vanderlip, Elihu Root, Thomas W. Lamont of the Morgans, Jacob Schiff, and J.P. Morgan. The formal sessions of the conference were organized around papers by Kemmerer, Laughlin, Johnson, Bush, Warburg, and Conant, and the general atmosphere was that bankers and businessmen were to take their general guidance from the attendant scholars. As James B. Forgan, Chicago banker who was now solidly in the central banking camp, put it: "Let the theorists, those who ... can study from past history and from present conditions the effect of what we are doing, lay down principles for us, and let us help them with the details." C. Stuart Patterson pointed to the great lessons of the Indianapolis Monetary Commission, and the way in which its proposals triumphed in action because "we went home and organized an aggressive and active movement." Patterson then laid down the marching orders of what this would mean concretely for the assembled troops:

---

[70] Livingston, *Origins*, p. 203.

That is just what you must do in this case, you must uphold the hands of Senator Aldrich. You have got to see that the bill which he formulates ... obtains the support of every part of this country.[71]

With the New York monetary conference over, it was now time for Aldrich, surrounded by a few of the topmost leaders of the financial elite, to go off in seclusion and hammer out a detailed plan around which all parts of the central bank movement could rally. Someone in the Aldrich inner circle, probably Morgan partner Henry P. Davison, got the idea of convening a small group of top leaders in a super-secret conclave to draft the central bank bill. On November 22, 1910, Senator Aldrich, with a handful of companions, set forth in a privately chartered railroad car from Hoboken, New Jersey, to the coast of Georgia, where they sailed to an exclusive retreat, the Jekyll Island Club on Jekyll Island, Georgia. Facilities for their meeting were arranged by club member and co-owner J.P. Morgan. The cover story released to the press was that this was a simple duck-hunting expedition, and the conferees took elaborate precautions on the trips there and back to preserve their secrecy. Thus, the attendees addressed each other only by first name, and the railroad car was kept dark and closed off from reporters or other travelers on the train. One reporter apparently caught on to the purpose of the meeting, but was in some way persuaded by Henry P. Davison to maintain silence.

The conferees worked for a solid week at Jekyll Island to hammer out the draft of the Federal Reserve bill. In addition to Aldrich, the conferees included Henry P. Davison, Morgan partner; Paul Warburg, whose address in the spring had greatly

---

[71] Ibid., pp. 205–07.

impressed Aldrich; Frank A. Vanderlip, vice president of the National City Bank of New York; and finally, A. Piatt Andrew, head of the NMC staff, who had recently been made assistant secretary of the Treasury by President Taft. After a week of meetings, the six men had forged a plan for a central bank, which eventually became the Aldrich Bill. Vanderlip acted as secretary of the meeting, and contributed the final writing.

The only substantial disagreement was tactical, with Aldrich attempting to hold out for a straightforward central bank on the European model, while Warburg and the other bankers insisted that the reality of central control be cloaked in the politically palatable camouflage of "decentralization." It is amusing that the bankers were the more politically astute, while the politician Aldrich wanted to waive political considerations. Warburg and the bankers won out, and the final draft was basically the Warburg plan with a decentralized patina taken from Morawetz.

The financial power elite now had a bill. The significance of the composition of the small meeting must be stressed: two Rockefeller men (Aldrich and Vanderlip), two Morgans (Davison and Norton), one Kuhn, Loeb person (Warburg), and one economist friendly to both camps (Andrew).[72]

After working on some revisions of the Jekyll Island draft with Forgan and George Reynolds, Aldrich presented the Jekyll Island draft as the Aldrich Plan to the full NMC in January 1911. But here an unusual event occurred. Instead of quickly presenting this Aldrich Bill to the Congress, its

---

[72] See Rothbard, "Federal Reserve," pp. 99–101; and Frank A. Vanderlip, *From Farm Boy to Financier* (New York: D. Appleton-Century, 1935), pp. 210–19.

drafters waited for a full year, until January 1912. Why the unprecedented year's delay?

The problem was that the Democrats swept the congressional elections in 1910, and Aldrich, disheartened, decided not to run for re-election to the Senate the following year. The Democratic triumph meant that the reformers had to devote a year of intensive agitation to convert the Democrats, and to intensify propaganda to the rest of banking, business, and the public. In short, the reformers needed to regroup and accelerate their agitation.

The Final Phase: Coping with the Democratic Ascendancy

The final phase of the drive for a central bank began in January 1911. At the previous January's meeting of the National Board of Trade, Paul Warburg had put through a resolution setting aside January 18, 1911, as a "monetary day" devoted to a "Business Men's Monetary Conference." This conference, run by the National Board of Trade, and featuring delegates from metropolitan mercantile organizations from all over the country, had C. Stuart Patterson as its chairman. The New York Chamber of Commerce, the Merchants' Association of New York, and the New York Produce Exchange, each of which had been pushing for banking reform for the previous five years, introduced a joint resolution to the monetary conference supporting the Aldrich Plan, and proposing the establishment of a new "businessmen's monetary reform league" to lead the public struggle for a central bank. After a speech in favor of the plan by A. Piatt Andrew, the entire conference adopted the resolution. In response, C. Stuart Patterson appointed none other than Paul M. Warburg to head a committee of seven to establish the reform league.

The committee of seven shrewdly decided, following the lead of the old Indianapolis convention, to establish the

National Citizens' League for the Creation of a Sound Banking System in Chicago rather than in New York, where the control really resided. The idea was to acquire the bogus patina of a "grassroots" heartland operation and to convince the public that the league was free of dreaded Wall Street control. As a result, the official heads of the league were Chicago businessmen John V. Farwell and Harry A. Wheeler, president of the U.S. Chamber of Commerce. The director was University of Chicago monetary economist J. Laurence Laughlin, assisted by his former student, Professor H. Parker Willis.

In keeping with its Midwestern aura, most of the directors of the Citizens' League were Chicago nonbanker industrialists: men such as B.E. Sunny of the Chicago Telephone Company, Cyrus McCormick of International Harvester (both companies in the Morgan ambit), John G. Shedd of Marshall Field and Company, Frederic A. Delano of the Wabash Railroad Company (Rockefeller-controlled), and Julius Rosenwald of Sears, Roebuck. Over a decade later, however, H. Parker Willis frankly conceded that the Citizens' League had been a propaganda organ of the nation's bankers.[73]

The Citizens' League swung into high gear during the spring and summer of 1911, issuing a periodical, *Banking and Reform*, designed to reach newspaper editors, and subsidizing pamphlets by such pro-reform experts as John Perrin,

---

[73] Henry Parker Willis, *The Federal Reserve System* (New York: Ronald Press, 1923), pp. 149–50. Willis's account, however, conveniently overlooks the dominating operational role that both he and his mentor Laughlin played in the Citizens' League. See Robert Craig West, *Banking Reform and the Federal Reserve, 1863–1923* (Ithaca, N.Y.: Cornell University Press, 1977), p. 82.

head of the American National Bank of Indianapolis, and George E. Roberts of the National City Bank of New York. Consultant on the newspaper campaign was H.H. Kohlsaat, former executive committee member of the Indianapolis Monetary Convention. Laughlin himself worked on a book on the Aldrich Plan, to be similar to his own report of 1898 for the Indianapolis convention.

Meanwhile, a parallel campaign was launched to bring the nation's bankers into camp. The first step was to convert the banking elite. For that purpose, the Aldrich inner circle organized a closed-door conference of 23 top bankers in Atlantic City in early February, which included several members of the currency commission of the American Bankers Association (ABA), along with bank presidents from nine leading cities of the country. After making a few minor revisions, the conference warmly endorsed the Aldrich Plan.

After this meeting, Chicago banker James B. Forgan, president of the Rockefeller-dominated First National Bank of Chicago, emerged as the most effective banker spokesman for the central bank movement. Not only was his presentation of the Aldrich Plan before the executive council of the ABA in May considered particularly impressive, it was especially effective coming from someone who had been a leading critic (if on relatively minor grounds) of the plan. As a result, the top bankers managed to get the ABA to violate its own bylaws and make Forgan chairman of its executive council.

At the Atlantic City conference, James Forgan had succinctly explained the purpose of the Aldrich Plan and of the conference itself. As Kolko sums up:

> the real purpose of the conference was to discuss winning the banking community over to government control

directly by the bankers for their own ends. ... It was generally appreciated that the [Aldrich Plan] would increase the power of the big national banks to compete with the rapidly growing state banks, help bring the state banks under control, and strengthen the position of the national banks in foreign banking activities.[74]

By November 1911, it was easy pickings to have the full American Bankers Association endorse the Aldrich Plan. The nation's banking community was now solidly lined up behind the drive for a central bank.

However, 1912 and 1913 were years of some confusion and backing and filling, as the Republican Party split between its insurgents and regulars, and the Democrats won increasing control over the federal government, culminating in Woodrow Wilson's gaining the presidency in the November 1912 elections. The Aldrich Plan, introduced into the Senate by Theodore Burton in January 1912, died a quick death, but the reformers saw that what they had to do was to drop the fiercely Republican partisan name of Aldrich from the bill, and with a few minor adjustments, rebaptize it as a Democratic measure. Fortunately for the reformers, this process of transformation was eased greatly in early 1912, when H. Parker Willis was appointed administrative assistant to Carter Glass, the Democrat from Virginia who now headed the House Banking and Currency Committee. In an accident of history, Willis had taught economics to the two sons of Carter Glass at Washington and Lee University, and they recommended him to their father when the Democrats assumed control of the House.

---

[74] Kolko, *Triumph*, p. 186.

The minutiae of the splits and maneuvers in the banking reform camp during 1912 and 1913, which have long fascinated historians, are fundamentally trivial to the basic story. They largely revolved around the successful efforts by Laughlin, Willis, and the Democrats to jettison the name Aldrich. Moreover, while the bankers had preferred the Federal Reserve Board to be appointed by the bankers themselves, it was clear to most of the reformers that this was politically unpalatable. They realized that the same result of a government-coordinated cartel could be achieved by having the president and Congress appoint the board, balanced by the bankers electing most of the officials of the regional Federal Reserve Banks, and electing an advisory council to the Fed. However, much would depend on whom the president would appoint to the board. The reformers did not have to wait long. Control was promptly handed to Morgan men, led by Benjamin Strong of Bankers Trust as all-powerful head of the Federal Reserve Bank of New York. The reformers had gotten the point by the end of congressional wrangling over the Glass bill, and by the time the Federal Reserve Act was passed in December 1913, the bill enjoyed overwhelming support from the banking community. As A. Barton Hepburn of the Chase National Bank persuasively told the American Bankers Association at its annual meeting of August 1913: "The measure recognizes and adopts the principles of a central bank. Indeed ... it will make all incorporated banks together joint owners of a central dominating power."[75] In fact, there was very little substantive difference between the

---

[75] Ibid., p. 235.

Aldrich and Glass bills: the goal of the bank reformers had been triumphantly achieved.[76, 77]

---

[76] On the essential identity of the two plans, see Friedman and Schwartz, *A Monetary History of the United States*, p. 171, n. 59; Kolko, Triumph, p. 235; and Paul M.Warburg, *The Federal Reserve System, Its Origins and Growth* (New York: Macmillan, 1930), 1, chaps. 8 and 9. On the minutiae of the various drafts and bills and the reactions to them, see West, *Banking Reform*, pp. 79–135; Kolko, *Triumph*, pp. 186–89, 217–47; and Livingston, *Origins*, pp. 217–26.

[77] On the capture of banking control in the new Federal Reserve System by the Morgans and their allies, and on the Morganesque policies of the Fed during the 1920s, see Rothbard, "Federal Reserve," pp. 103–36.

Conclusion

The financial elites of this country, notably the Morgan, Rockefeller, and Kuhn, Loeb interests, were responsible for putting through the Federal Reserve System, as a governmentally created and sanctioned cartel device to enable the nation's banks to inflate the money supply in a coordinated fashion, without suffering quick retribution from depositors or noteholders demanding cash. Recent researchers, however, have also highlighted the vital supporting role of the growing number of technocratic experts and academics, who were happy to lend the patina of their allegedly scientific expertise to the elites' drive for a central bank. To achieve a regime of big government and government control, power elites cannot achieve their goal of privilege through statism without the vital legitimizing support of the supposedly disinterested experts and the professoriat. To achieve the Leviathan state, interests seeking special privilege, and intellectuals offering scholarship and ideology, must work hand in hand.

Index

Academy of Political Science (APS), 77n, 80, 91

Adams, Brooks, 42, 43n, 47

Adams, Henry, 42

Adams, Thomas S., 56n

Aldrich, Nelson W., 37, 83, 84–85, 87, 89, 93–95

    Aldrich Bill, 37, 83, 94

    Aldrich Plan, 94, 97, 99–101

    Aldrich-Vreeland Act, 83

    Jekyll Island retreat, 93–94

    National Monetary Commission (NMC), 83–85, 88–89, 91–92, 94

Allison, William Boyd, 27

American Academy of Political and Social Science (AAPSS), 80, 82, 89

American Bankers Association (ABA), 36–37, 74–75, 84, 86, 99–101

American Economic Association (AEA), 28, 48, 50–52, 70, 86

American Telephone and Telegraph Company (AT&T), 26, 38n

Andrew, Abram Piatt, 73, 85, 89, 94, 97

Baker, George F., 38, 72–73, 85

Bankers Magazine, 35, 72n, 78

Banking

    branches and cartelization, 37

    commercial paper, 76, 90

country banks, 25, 36–38, 82, 87

decentralized banking, 76, 81–82, 87

demand deposits, 12

national banking system, 12–13, 35, 86–87

unhappiness with, 11–14

National Banking Acts, 12

Peel's Bank Act of 1844, 36n

"pet banks," 39

problems, 89

See also Banks; Credit expansion

Bank(s)

Bank of England, 35n, 85

central banks, 71, 80, 92–94

academic organizations and, 89

acquiring legitimacy for, 73

drive for, 71

lender of last resort, 12, 79, 86

legislative activity for, 83

secret conclave to draft plans for, 92–93

First National Bank of Chicago, 30, 75, 86, 99

Kuhn, Loeb, 14, 20, 22, 48n, 65, 71–73, 75, 77, 84, 94, 103

central bank proponent, 14, 71

Rockefeller-Harriman-Kuhn, Loeb, 20

Barrows, David P., 60n

Bimetallism, 53–54, 57, 63

fallacies of, 54

Birmingham, Stephen, 48n, 72n

Boxer Rebellion, 64

Bretton Woods Agreement, 41–42, 68

Bryan, William Jennings, 15

Bryanism, 16, 25

Bureau of Insular Affairs (BIA), 56–57

Burton, Theodore, 84, 87, 100

Bush, Irving T., 86, 92

Bush, Thomas G., 22

Businessmen's Monetary Reform League, 97

Butler, Nicholas Murray, 80

Cartelization of banking industry, 12

Carver, Thomas Nixon, 73, 86

Central banks. See Banks

Chapman, S.J., 44

Chicago Times-Herald, 18

Chicago Tribune, 35

Claflin, John, 73

Clark, John Bates, 47, 82

Cline, Virgil P., 26

Conant, Charles A., 24–25, 28n, 29, 35, 43–45, 47, 56–59, 61–64, 66–69, 73, 75, 82, 85, 88–89, 91–92

    Conant plan, 57, 59

    "conants," 59, 63

    currency reforms, 69

    failure in Cuba and China, 62–63

    surplus capital, theory of, 43, 46, 88

Consolidated Gas Company of New York, 38n

Converse, Edmund C., 19

Credit expansion

    controlled by large national banks, 76

    See also Banks

Cumberland, William W., 70

Currency Report, 74

Czarist Russia, 45

Davison, Henry P., 85, 93–94

Dean, William B., 22

Democratic Party

    end of *laissez-faire* libertarian party, 15

Dewey, Commodore, 45

Dewey, Davis R., 86

Dewey, John, 86

Discount rate, 74, 88

Dodge, William E., 23, 52

Duffield, J.R., 83

Eames, Henry F., 26

Economist, as "social scientist," 48

Edmunds, George F., 21

Elasticity

    "elastic," 20, 25, 28, 33, 71–71, 81–81, 88

    "inelastic," 13, 16, 36, 73, 81, 91

Eliot, Charles, 85

Ely, Robert E., 89

Fairchild, Charles S., 22, 26

Fairchild, Sidney T., 22

Farwell, John V., 98

Faulkner, Roland P., 56n

Federal Reserve Bank, 101

 favors granted to large banks, 86

 origins of, 16–17, 41

 spurious veil of regionalism, 87

Fiat money. *See* Money

Field, Marshall, 26, 98

Financial elites

 advising governments, science of, 67

 force behind Fed creation, 103

Fish, Stuyvesant, 22

Fisher, Irving, 86

Forgan, James B., 75

Founding Fathers, 44

Fowler Bill, 36–37, 71

Fowler, Charles N., 36

Gage, Lyman J., 30, 33, 35, 39–40, 72–73

Garnett, Louis A., 22

Gavitt, J.P., 89

General Electric, 20, 22

German Historical School, 48

German Reichsbank, 86, 90

Glass, Carter, 100

Gold coin, 63

Gold standard
    Act of 1900, 33
    fixed relationship between countries, 60
    reformers and, 33
Gould, Jay, 52
Government
    big government, 11
    debt and surplus capital with, 88
Government-bank-press complex created, 88
Great Depression, 42
Gresham's Law, 57, 63

Hadley, Arthur Twining, 27–28, 49, 51
Hamlin, Charles S., 50
Hanna, Hugh Henry, 17–18, 24, 29–30, 33, 61
Hanna, Mark, 15, 19, 30, 75
Harding, Warren G., 14n, 75
Harrison, Charles Custis, 18
Hentz, Henry, 23
Hepburn, A. Barton, 29, 36, 75, 82, 101
Herrick, Myron T., 75
Hoarding, 79
Hobson, John A., 43n
Hollander, Jacob H., 55, 56n, 58, 65, 69
Hutzler, Abraham, 65

Imperialism, 42–46, 49–50, 52–54, 55n, 56, 58, 59n, 60n, 64, 66
    consent of governed, 44

economic benefits of, 45

increased centralization of administrative power, 49–50

sponsors of, 52

surplus capital and, 42

Indianapolis Board of Trade, 17

Indianapolis Monetary Convention, 18–20, 25, 33–34, 37–38, 73, 99

Inflation

general assets, as base of, 74

International Harvester, 98

International monetary order, 68

Interstate Commerce Commission, 9, 11

Jekyll Island

Fed bill drafted at, 93

Jenks, Jeremiah W., 27, 28n, 50, 58–59, 61, 64–65, 69–70

Johnson, Joseph French, 35–36, 73, 89, 91–92

Kemmerer, Edwin W., 59, 69–70, 91–92

Kent, Fred I., 85, 89, 91

Kuhn, Loeb. *See* Banks

Laissez-faire, 7–9, 16, 46, 48, 55

Lamont, Thomas W., 92

Laughlin, James Laurence, 22–23, 28–29, 92, 98–99, 101

Lehrman, Lewis, 13n

Leighton, George, 22

Lenin, Vladimir, 42–43

capitalist imperialism theory, 42

Limantour, Jose, 60, 63

Lodge, Henry Cabot, 15, 42

Loeb, Guta, 48n

Loeb, Nina, 48n, 72n

Loeb, Solomon, 72n

MacVeagh, Franklin, 26

Magoon, Charles, 63

Mahan, Alfred T., 42

Marburg, Theodore, 52

Marxism, 9, 81

McKinley, William, 14n, 15–16, 18–21, 25, 30, 33, 39, 75

Merchants' Association of New York, 91, 92, 97

Mexican Currency Reform Act of 1905, 63

Mitchell, John J., 18

Monetary imperialism, 53, 58, 64

Monetary reform

      movement of 1896–1900, 15–34

      first monetary convention, 17–25

      passage, Gold Standard Act, 33–35

      second monetary convention, 25–29

Money

      debasement, 54, 57, 64

      demand for, 34, 91

      fiat, 12, 68

      hard, 11, 15, 16

      medium of exchange, 62

Monopoly

    government-imposed, 8

    redefined, 8–9

Morawetz, Victor, 77, 87, 94

Morgan, J.P., "Jack," 11, 20, 22-23, 26, 36, 38, 56, 73, 82, 85, 87, 92, 93

    House of Morgan

        influence of, 7, 8, 13-16, 18-20, 26-27, 38, 39, 42, 50, 52, 56, 69, 72-75, 84-86, 87n, 89, 92-94, 98, 101, 102n, 103

        political power and, 13

National Citizens' League for the Creation of a Sound Banking System, 98

National Monetary Commission (NMC), 83–85, 88–89, 91–92, 94

New York Chamber of Commerce, 71, 73, 75, 92, 97

New York Journal of Commerce, 35

North American Review, 44

Ocean Herald, 18

Open market purchases, 30, 39

Orr, Alexander E., 18, 20, 23

Overstreet, Jesse, 29

Panic of 1907, 79, 80–81

    launch of drive for central bank, 80

Patterson, C. Stuart, 18, 21, 92, 97

Payne, Henry C., 19–20

Peabody, George Foster, 19–21, 23

Perkins, Charles E., 27

Perrin, John, 98

Pillsbury, C.A., 26

Plehn, Carl C., 60n

Political Science Quarterly, 35n, 48

Pope, Alfred A., 26

Populists, 15–16

Pratt, Sereno S., 83

Progressive Era, 7, 11, 49

Pullman Company, 18, 38n

Purves, Alexander, 39

Purchasing Power, 42

Putnam, George Haven, 28n

Railroads

      Atchison, Topeka and Santa Fe Railway, 28, 77, 87n

      Birmingham Railroad, 22

      Erie Railroad, 18, 38n

      Missouri Pacific Railroad, 22

      New York Central Railroad, 22, 38n, 51

      Chicago Railroad, 18–19

Recession

      always follows boom, 12

      bank credit increased in, 25, 30, 39

      of 1907, 79

Reform of the Currency, 90

Review of Reviews, 28n, 50

Reynolds, Arthur, 74

Reynolds, George M., 74, 85–87, 94

Ridgely, William B., 38, 82

Roberts, George E., 82, 89, 99

Rockefeller, John D., Jr., 37n, 83

Rockefeller, John D., Sr., 18–19, 23, 26, 30, 37–38, 72, 75, 83, 89

Rockefeller, Nelson Aldrich, 37n

Rockefeller, William, 38

Roosevelt, Franklin D., 14n

Roosevelt, Theodore, 14n, 19, 27, 39, 42, 50, 59–60, 64, 85

Root, L. Carroll, 23

Root, Elihu, 56, 64, 82, 92

Rosenwald, Julius, 98

Say's Law, 43

Schiff, Jacob, 71–73, 75–76, 85, 92

Seager, Henry R., 86

Sears, Roebuck and Company, 98

Seligman, Isaac N., 52

Seligman, Edwin R.A., 48, 50, 52, 80–81, 86, 91

Shaw, Dr. Albert, 50

Shaw, Leslie M., 26–27, 38–40, 71, 73

Shearman, Thomas, 52

Shedd, John G., 98

Shelton, Arthur B., 89

Silva, Edward T., 49n, 50–51, 56n, 60n

Sound Currency, 24

Spain, 43, 45, 54

Specie

    payment, suspension of, 28, 79

    See also Money

Sprague, Albert A., 26

Sprague, Oliver M.W., 86

Springfield (Mass.) Republican, 46

Stahlman, E.B., 19

Stanard, Edwin O., 18

Standard Oil Company, 20, 26

Stetson, Francis Lynde, 82, 87n

Stillman, James, 38, 72

Stock market

acceptance program and, 77n

Straus, Isidore, 73

Strauss, Albert, 73

Strobel, Edward R., 50

Strong, Reverend Josiah, 47

Sunny, B.E., 98

Taft, William Howard, 14n, 75, 87, 94

Talbert, Joseph T., 75

Taussig, Frank W., 27–28, 34, 86

Taylor, Frank M., 27–28

Taylor, Robert S., 22, 29

Third World countries

exploitation of, 56–57

imposition of gold-exchange standard on, 66

victims of imperialism, 53

Transportation, 18, 26

Trask, Spencer, 21

U.S. Chamber of Commerce, 98

U.S. Investor, 43n, 45

U.S. Treasury, 37

       as central bank, 30, 37, 39, 57, 71, 73

       Independent Treasury System, 39

Vanderlip, Frank A., 35, 38, 72–73, 75–76, 81–82, 85, 92, 94

Wade, Festus J., 84

Wall Street Journal, 81, 83, 88–89

War(s)

       of 1898, theory of imperialism, 43

       Spanish-American War, 43, 45, 49

World War I, 63, 85

Warburg, Paul Moritz, 48n, 72, 77, 82, 85–86, 90–94, 97, 102n

       central bank, leader in fight for, 77–94

       Jekyll Island retreat, 93

Wetmore, Charles W., 19

Wheeler, Harry A., 98

Wheelock, Thomas, 81

White, Horace, 89

Willcox, W.H., 55n

Willis, Henry Parker, 23, 98, 100–01

Willoughby, William F., 56n

Willson, A.E., 19

Wilshire, H. Gaylord, 43n

Wilson, Woodrow, 14n, 65n, 87n, 100

Wilson administration, 20

Wood, Leonard, 62
Wood, Stuart, 52
Young, Arthur N., 70

Made in the USA
Coppell, TX
10 June 2020